GoldenEye 007

GoldenEye 007

Alyse Knorr

Boss Fight Books
Los Angeles, CA
bossfightbooks.com

ISBN 13: 978-1-940535-29-6
First Printing: 2022

Series Editor: Gabe Durham
Associate Editor: Michael P. Williams
Book Design by Cory Schmitz
Page Design by Christopher Moyer

For Kate

CONTENTS

MISSION BRIEFING

A HEARTBEAT POUNDS OVER AN ominous low tone as a 3D Nintendo logo spins on screen. Echoey percussion builds the suspense until suddenly the James Bond theme song kicks in and the film franchise's iconic opening gun barrel sequence begins. A tuxedo-pixelated Bond strides into frame, turns to the camera, and shoots. Red blood spills over the lens. The same red blood that will cascade down your screen each time you die—and you will, often—in this game, *GoldenEye 007* for the Nintendo 64 (N64).

When *GoldenEye* debuted in August of 1997, it was a revelation. Just a year prior, N64 owners had been wowed by the fully 3D world of *Super Mario 64*, endlessly frustrated by *Star Wars: Shadows of the Empire* and its snowspeeder's goddamn tow cables, and delighted by the multiplayer frenzy of *Mario Kart 64*. But *GoldenEye* was a different breed of game altogether. It took over high-school sleepovers and college dorm parties and proved just how much fun the N64's four controller ports could really be. It was the first first-person shooter (FPS) many of us ever played, introducing a generation of console gamers to a whole new world of grown-up gaming. *GoldenEye* is still synonymous with the 1990s for many Millennial gamers, calling up nostalgic memories of those last years of a simpler, quainter century, before 9/11, before the fallout of Columbine and near-daily mass shootings. *GoldenEye* was both a rite of passage into adulthood and the last game of our collective era of innocence—a game as silly as it was violent, an artifact of another time.

Based on the 1995 James Bond movie of the same name, *GoldenEye* not only recreates the film's narrative but expands on it in twenty different missions spanning from Russia to Monaco to Cuba, each tersely labeled with a one-word name signifying its setting: Dam, Runway, Jungle, Archives. Gameplay operates from the first-person perspective of Bond himself, and all of the film's major allies and villains appear as characters, along with a vast army of enemy soldiers and guards you have to either stealthily sneak past or ruthlessly murder to make your way through each level.

Every mission begins with a briefing, displayed on file dossiers like something straight out of MI6 headquarters, featuring advice from Bond's boss M, gadget specialist Q, and office flirt Moneypenny. The objectives in any given mission range from stealing secret documents to rescuing hostages to planting explosives, and everything in between. In *GoldenEye*, each level feels entirely new but always satisfyingly Bond-like. When you die in the game, you have to watch a cinematic, slow-motion reenactment of your death; when you beat a level, you get to see a report of your gameplay statistics: number of shots fired, number of enemies killed, firing accuracy, etc. Bond is, after all, a professional.

GoldenEye's visual and audio effects felt state-of-the-art for the era, allowing a level of interactivity and immersion that no game had ever attempted before. You could write your name on the wall with bullet holes, shatter a sheet of glass while sniping a guard in a tower, and hop into a tank and run over screaming soldiers. Civilians put their hands up, knees shaking, when you pointed a gun at them. The game's many different weapons all shot at different rates, with different sound effects and accuracy metrics, and reloaded with a satisfying click. And for the first time in a video game, enemies winced in pain at whichever specific body part you shot.

Playing *GoldenEye* just felt good—from the thrill of sneaking up on a Siberian commando and taking him out with a satisfying "pew pew" from your silenced PP7 pistol, to the tension of sprinting through a missile silo just before launch while a countdown ticks away on your screen. For every climactic boss battle and loud firefight (*everything* in this game explodes when you shoot it—even tables and chairs), there were also quiet moments of slipping, spy-like, down the hall of an enemy base, covertly employing gadgets to steal classified information.

GoldenEye was a commercial hit and a creative masterpiece, blending together an odd mixture of influences from arcade games, racing games, maze shooters, and John Woo action movies. Its quirks and idiosyncrasies have become beloved points of gaming lore, and its gameplay mechanics, particularly around stealth and multiplayer, continue to influence present-day first-person shooters. But by all accounts, *GoldenEye* should never have been a success. At the time it debuted, console first-person shooters weren't popular at all, and games based on movies were usually seen as tacky tie-ins at best. Only two members of *GoldenEye*'s eight-man development team had ever worked on a game before, and they missed deadline after deadline until the title debuted a whopping two years after its movie namesake.

In a prophetic review of the game just after its release, an *N64 Magazine* writer predicted that "*GoldenEye* will take the world by storm, and the features it introduces will be copied by game designers everywhere. While they're busy copying, they'll forget *GoldenEye*'s finest and most important quality—that for all the visual and aural perfection, it's the game that's the lifeblood of it all. Nobody does it better." But how did a game made by a team of complete rookies, against all odds, become the lifeblood of an entire genre?

KILLER INSTINCTS
AND A SWAGGER

IN 1995, NINTENDO'S PRESIDENT, Hiroshi Yamauchi, purchased the licensing rights to adapt the yet-unreleased *GoldenEye* film, or "Bond 17," as it was known at the time, into a game. Nintendo's top leadership knew right away which developer to entrust with the license. Rare, a scrappy, homegrown British studio and Nintendo's favorite developer, had already, after fifteen years in existence, made a name in video gaming. And who better to take on a game starring a British cultural icon than a company based in England?

But when Nintendo approached Rare's upper management to ask if they wanted to make a game based on the next Bond film, Rare's founding co-presidents, a pair of 30-something-year-old brothers named Tim and Chris Stamper, responded with, "Well, not really." The brothers were wary of how a film tie-in game could limit their creative freedom, and creative freedom had always been of paramount importance to them—it's why they had left their jobs in arcade games and started their own company back in 1982.

The Stamper brothers' talent had shined from an early age. Chris started tinkering with electronics as a young boy and eventually built his own computer in college. He got his first programming job—in arcade games—before he had even graduated. Meanwhile, Tim brought to the table an artistic eye and a knack for graphic design. Uncanny business sense combined with excellent creative instincts and big dreams had led the Stamper brothers to enormous success in their earliest days as a company, when they produced games under the trading name "Ultimate Play the Game," chosen because, in Tim's words, "it was representative of our products: the ultimate games."

In May 1983, Ultimate's very first release—a 2D shooting platformer called *Jetpac*—hit it big on the ZX Spectrum home computer, selling 300,000 copies. Considering about one million people owned a Spectrum at the time, this was, in Chris's words, "incredible penetration for a single product." The Stampers worked insane hours to make this happen—eighteen-hour days, seven days per week. In fact, they only took off two days from work over the course of three years—both Christmas mornings.

The brothers' efforts won them a Golden Joystick award for Best Software House in 1983 and 1984 and a slew of critical and commercial hit games for the ZX Spectrum, including *Atic Atac* (1983), *Lunar Jetman*

(1983), *Sabre Wulf* (1984), and *Knight Lore* (1984), a game that the gaming magazine *Edge*, ten years later, called possibly "the greatest single advance in the history of computer games" thanks to its revolutionary isometric graphics that looked 3D. *Knight Lore* was so ahead of its time that the Stampers had to delay its release until after *Sabre Wulf*, even though *Knight Lore* was finished first, because they feared the game would raise expectations so quickly that it would be impossible to sell *Sabre Wulf*.

The quality of Ultimate's games stood out—in particular, their cutting-edge graphics and fun, well-designed gameplay. The Stampers generally let powerful technology lead the way; their previous experience in arcade games offered them useful knowledge in both hardware design and software writing, and while everyone else wrote their games in BASIC machine code, the Stampers wrote theirs in Z80, which meant that their games ran much faster.

Simply put, Ultimate made some of the best games in the UK and was already a household name by 1983. They were one of the first British game companies to earn that kind of brand recognition and one of the first to develop their own fanbase. Spectrum owners worshipped Ultimate, whose fame reached a "Beatles-scale fandom," according to journalist Eric-Jon Rössel Waugh. In fact, Ultimate received so much fan mail in their early years—up to 60 letters per day—that they had to employ someone just to manage it.

Adding to Ultimate's allure was their legendary elusiveness. The Stampers quickly grew famous for how private they were—they didn't go to trade shows or conferences and rarely granted interviews with the media. Ultimate's isolated rural headquarters featured an entry phone, thick tinted windows, and "Private: Keep Out" signs on the garage. The message was clear: Ultimate didn't need fancy PR—the games spoke for themselves.

Then, just when it had reached the peak of its fame, Ultimate Play the Game disappeared completely. In 1985, the Stampers sold Ultimate and its entire catalogue of games and moved to Twycross, England, a small village in the middle of nowhere with a famous zoo and not much else. Ultimate's sudden disappearance shocked the gaming community—it seemed they had vanished as quickly and mysteriously as they had appeared. But the truth is that the Stampers had been carefully planning Ultimate's disappearance. In order to prevent their next big project from getting controlled by a buyout of Ultimate, the Stampers had quietly set up a new subsidiary company. After flipping through a thesaurus—the way they titled all their games—the Stampers decided to name their new company "Rare Designs of the Future," or "Rare" for short.

After a trip to Tokyo at the end of 1983, a business partner of the Stampers had sent them a Nintendo Famicom (later released as the Nintendo Entertainment System or NES in the West) and encouraged them to develop for it, telling them he thought it was the future of gaming. The Stampers hesitated at first, and for good reason. Nintendo hadn't yet begun exporting the Famicom outside of Japan, and most British game developers had their eyes set on the upcoming wave of 16-bit computers like the Atari ST and Commodore Amiga. Abandoning the wildly popular Spectrum for a totally unknown Japanese machine would be a risky move for the Stampers, but they had lofty goals, and refused to limit themselves with provincial thinking.

So, under their secret Rare subdivision, Chris set to work studying the Famicom. After Nintendo denied his requests for the machine's programming code, he spent eight months reverse-engineering it himself. When the brothers finally snagged a meeting with Nintendo of America president Minoru Arakawa, they became the first Western company to ever pitch Nintendo. The Stampers ended up impressing the company so much with their demo project—a skiing game called *Slalom* (1986)—that Nintendo gave Rare an official license and an unlimited budget to make games on a freelance basis. Rare had become Nintendo's first Western third-party developer, thus beginning the relationship that would eventually lead to *GoldenEye*.

Between 1986 and 1991, Rare produced 60 games for the Game Boy and NES, including many film, TV, and comic licensed games like *Wheel of Fortune*, *Hollywood Squares*, and *Who Framed Roger Rabbit?* They worked on a huge variety of titles, from wrestling games to racing games to platformers and even a tarot card simulator. Rare also ported a number of PC, arcade, and pinball games to the NES, which let the Stampers closely study the principles of Japanese game design.

By 1991, Nintendo dominated all regions and outsourced more and more of their game production to third-party developers like Rare. In June of 1991, Rare launched *Battletoads*, an original NES game whose brash amphibian protagonists were intended to rival the Teenage Mutant Ninja Turtles. The game's three muscley toad heroes—Rash, Pimple, and Zitz—charmed players, as did the title's innovative approaches to co-op modes, animation, and music. With features like parallax levels, different scroll settings, and a mixture of gameplay styles in one cartridge (racing, platformer, and combat), *Battletoads* squeezed out every last drop of the NES's hardware potential toward the end of its life. Rare had more than established their claim as Nintendo's favorite developer—but they were about to make an even bolder move.

Endless ambition drove the Stampers to keep innovating, and they saw an opportunity to break new ground in 3D game graphics. And so the Stamper brothers pooled together the profits they'd made over the previous years and made a risky investment in the largest bank of expensive Silicon Graphics computers in Britain—enough to make them one of the most technologically advanced developers in the world.

The Stampers harnessed the power of their SG machines—the same technology used to render textured

3D models in the films *Jurassic Park* and *Terminator 2*—to produce cutting-edge, 3D-looking graphics. Rare's innovative approach, called Advanced Computer Modeling, incorporated motion capture, light sourcing, and photorealistic graphics to make the most dazzling visuals in the games industry. After seeing a demonstration of Rare's amazing new techniques, Nintendo decided to entrust the company with a killer app for the 16-bit Super Nintendo Entertainment System (SNES). They even dusted off a famous out-of-use character from their back catalogue to star in Rare's platformer: Donkey Kong, the very character that had first made Nintendo famous in the arcade world.

When *Donkey Kong Country* debuted in 1994, it blew the world away with its gorgeous graphics, which somehow made a 16-bit game look 3D. *Donkey Kong Country* sold a whopping eight million copies, making it the best-selling SNES game not bundled with the SNES and the third overall best-selling SNES game. The title was such a hit that it ensured Nintendo's victory in the 1990s console sales war against Sega by keeping the 16-bit SNES relevant even after 32-bit consoles like Sony's PlayStation had entered the market.

After *Donkey Kong Country*, Rare slowed down their pace and made fewer games at a time. "I'd rather see one single high-quality game than ten low-quality games," Tim Stamper said at the time, clearly having internalized Nintendo's mantra of quality over quantity. In 1995,

Rare released *Diddy's Kong Quest*, a sequel to *Donkey Kong Country* that was even better than the original.

By the time the *GoldenEye* license came along in 1995, Rare enjoyed a treasured ten-year relationship with Nintendo. An IGN writer described the partnership like this: "[Rare is] Nintendo's best friend and its most important companion. Whenever the Kyoto giant is in need for some quality products to fill in between its scarce releases, Rare comes to the rescue." And so, after its symbolic investment in Rare via Donkey Kong, Nintendo put its money where its mouth was and purchased a 25% stake in the British developer in April 1995 for a grand total of $39.5 million. The purchase marked Nintendo's first-ever investment in a Western software developer. Nintendo eventually upped their stake in the company to 49%, making them Rare's primary shareholder after the Stampers, who owned the other 51% to ensure Rare remained an independent company. At this point, Rare had not only become Nintendo's first-ever second-party developer, but had also become a publisher.

Rare now had the resources they needed to take big risks, and with Nintendo's backing and new talent arriving at their campus all the time, the stage was set for one of Rare's most ambitious games yet.

•

Tucked away like a gem in quiet, rural Twycross, Rare's company headquarters in 1995 provided the perfect setting for developing great games. The remote location ensured total focus, and security cameras (which later inspired the ones surveilling the grounds of *GoldenEye*'s Russian bases) guaranteed total privacy. The site even had its own canteen, where employees could wolf down 30-minute lunches before heading back to work. But the Twycross studio did have one big problem—parking. After the Nintendo investment launched a huge company expansion, fitting all the cars in the cramped lot felt "literally like completing a jigsaw puzzle," a former employee noted, with young new employees squishing their Ford Fiestas in around the Ferraris and Lamborghinis of the veteran staffers.

One of *GoldenEye*'s composers, Grant Kirkhope, said that at Rare during the 1990s, it felt like everything they touched turned to gold. But even though Rare was an international powerhouse, it also remained at its heart a family company in a tiny, isolated village. The Stampers' mother cooked in the canteen, their sister did the wages, their other brother served as a groundskeeper, and their father drove employees to and from the airport. Rare was still small enough that Tim and Chris actually worked on games in addition to managing the company, though this changed during the two and a half years of *GoldenEye*'s development. At the beginning of the game's development period, Rare employed only about 40 people; after *GoldenEye*'s release, the total staff had blossomed to more than 100.

In 1994, one of Rare's newest talents was Martin Hollis, hired out of college as a programmer. In photos from the era, Hollis looks almost unbearably young in his black T-shirt and pants, with his long hair tied back in a ponytail and a sweet, shy smile flickering on his lips. Hollis is a slim man with a gracious, unpretentious demeanor. He speaks thoughtfully and deliberately, with infectious enthusiasm for any topic. Hollis has a whip-smart, eclectic sense of humor, evidenced in a Twitter account where he might write the dark "Borges" version of a *Time* article one day and an analysis of the intro to *Friends* another.

Growing up, Hollis always enjoyed making things. He spent his childhood playing with Legos, building sandcastles, and playing games like *Knight Lore*—which was made, of course, by his future bosses. Hollis's first encounter with a computer changed his life forever. Because his father was a teacher, Hollis had special access to the school's Acorn BBC Micro computers, which came with a manual that included a circuit diagram. And so, at the age of twelve, Hollis started not only playing games on the Micro, but writing them as well. "At the time, you had to copy or print out whole pages of programming code and enter them into the computer to play a game or use a program," Hollis said in 2016. "I tried my hand at writing programs and read tons of books about the [BBC Micro]. I ended up creating a lot of games (between 20 and 40). Some were published in magazines, others were actually released, and all before my 16th birthday."

Hollis developed his programming skills amidst a much bigger British home-coding boom. Thousands of self-taught, usually male teen programmers tinkered away throughout Britain in the 80s, including Tim and Chris Stamper and several other members of the *GoldenEye* team. This generation of "bedroom coders," as they came to be known, developed their skills thanks to a nationwide computer literacy program sponsored in part by the BBC to make Britain the world's most computer-literate country. Hollis went on to study computer science at Cambridge, in the world's very first computer science program; when Hollis joined Rare's staff, he was their first-ever computer science graduate.

Hollis spent his first year at Rare working on the 1994 arcade fighting game *Killer Instinct*, and he found Rare's culture of technical innovation thrilling. Hollis loved working on the powerful SG machines and learning about hardware, but he wasn't only a technophile—he also had a fundamental love of games, particularly artistic, innovative, and simple emergent games like *Tetris*.

By November 1994, Hollis was finishing up work on *Killer Instinct*. He had little serious influence on the game during its eleven-month development period (although he told me he did come up with the game's title), and he wasn't interested in working on the game's SNES port. As he read up about the "Ultra 64," Nintendo's new console in development, he heard a rumor around the office that Rare had been offered the Bond license but would likely turn it down.

Hollis, a Bond fan who as a child once made a home video recreating the iconic Bond intro sequence, was eager to take on the project. In early 1995, he approached Tim Stamper and asked if he could spearhead the Bond game himself. "I said to Tim Stamper, 'This sounds cool, I'd like to make this game,'" Hollis explained in 2012. Stamper asked Hollis to write a game design document, and in February 1995, Hollis told me, he drafted "a couple of scrappy pages of big thoughts." By April, these thoughts had evolved into a neatly typed nine-page game design document (the first he'd ever written) that convinced Stamper and the rest of Rare management to grant the project a full green light. "I can't really explain why they had trust in me after simply being second programmer on *Killer Instinct*, but I'm delighted and honored that they did," Hollis said in 2012.

The fact that the game was licensed from a film neither scared nor excited Hollis, who was unaware of the stigma around licensed games. "Thinking back, I could have thought one of two things," he said later. "I could have thought 'Oh boy, movie-to-game conversions suck.' But I didn't. Alternatively, I could have thought 'Ker-ching! Bond is a great franchise. This game will sell and sell!' But I didn't. I wasn't really focused on the business side of things at that time, I was just focused on making the game great. Instead of these things, I thought 'Bond: cool!'"

•

During his nearly 60 years on screen, James Bond has grown to become more than just a character or even a franchise. At this point, Bond is an idea. A brand. An industry. In the words of two noteworthy Bond scholars, Bond is, globally, "the most popular—in the sense of widely known—figure of the post-war period, if not of this century." Bond has survived adaptations from books to films to games and music. His intertextuality extends beyond even these genres into advertisements and merchandise ranging from toys and clothes to liquor and guns. As a subject of scholarly study, Bond has been interpreted as a mummy, a cyborg, a lesbian icon (seriously), and a source of anal fixation. In one Bond studies anthology, there's a whole article titled simply, "James Bond's Penis."

Bond was invented by Ian Fleming, a British journalist from a well-to-do family who served as a naval intelligence officer during WWII. After the war, Fleming decided to pursue his longtime ambition of writing a spy novel, in part to distract himself from his highly fraught upcoming marriage. He published his first Bond novel, *Casino Royale*, in 1953, never expecting his books would become bestsellers. Fleming went on to write fourteen Bond novels total, all at his paradise Jamaican vacation home Goldeneye, which he named after a real-life WWII military operation he'd helped plan and which went on to inspire the name of the film and game.[1] "Fleming could never have imagined what [Bond] was going to become," Bond scholar Jeremy Strong told me in an interview for this book. The first Bond movie, *Dr. No*, premiered in 1962 and was followed by 23 more films, debuting like clockwork every year or two. The Bond franchise is the longest-running series in cinema history and the third-highest-grossing film series of all time at $7 billion to date.

That's a lot of cash to spend on a character that Fleming once admitted he crafted as "an extremely dull, uninteresting man to whom things happened." Fleming settled on the name "James Bond" because he thought it was "the dullest name [he'd] ever heard," he said—fitting for a hero he thought of less as a complex individual and more as "a blunt instrument." Of course, no one ever accused Bond of having an interesting personality (or a personality at all)—he's more like an empty avatar into which the audience can insert themselves; an affectless, stiff-lipped shell of masculinity like the cowboy and

1 This means that *GoldenEye* the game was named after a movie named after a villa named after a military operation named after either Carson McCullers' 1941 novel *Reflections in a Golden Eye* or a type of duck called the Goldeneye (Fleming was an avid birdwatcher).

samurai before him, and a caricature of imperialist exceptionalism.

The Bond fantasy, Strong pointed out to me, is all about being the best at everything: guns, women, cars, and even cigars and food—in the books, Bond always knows the best place to get lunch in any given city in the world. As sexist and imperialist as it is, Bond's particular brand of superlative escapism embodies the power fantasy of the FPS genre, where players want to feel like the best and most badass at everything they do.

But Hollis couldn't rely on the Bond name alone to make a good game. In fact, many horrible Bond games preceded *GoldenEye*. The first Bond games were card, board, and tabletop role-playing games, and their marketing relied on the selling point that the player got to *be* Bond. No matter how well Bond resonated with film audiences, however, Bond games struggled to achieve quality and success, perhaps because of the inherent difficulty of translating films (something you passively watch) into games (something you actively participate in).

To make matters worse, in 1995, when production began on *GoldenEye* the movie, Bond had sunk to his least popular moment in history, putting the entire franchise in jeopardy. Bond's studio, MGM, was struggling financially after accumulating a ton of debt. Under US banking laws, the nearly bankrupt studio had to find a buyer fast, so they desperately needed a hit film to get someone interested. A lawsuit over distribution rights had left a troublingly long six-year gap since the last Bond movie, *License to Kill* (1989). This film and its predecessor, *The Living Daylights* (1987) had both starred Timothy Dalton, the least popular Bond ever.

Even Martin Campbell, *GoldenEye*'s director, doubted at first whether he even wanted to direct a Bond movie: "I questioned whether Bond was part of the 90s or an anachronism," he later explained. Sexism and imperialism no longer looked as cool as they might have in the 1960s, and now that the Cold War had ended, who did James Bond have left to fight? With the press and the film's own director questioning the series's relevance, *GoldenEye* also faced stiff competition from other very popular rival action series that had debuted during Bond's six-year absence, like Lethal Weapon and Die Hard.

With expectations for its film namesake this low, the prospects for *GoldenEye* the game seemed to be in the basement. Hollis was starting work on a project no one at Rare had wanted based on a film that the general public didn't seem excited about.

Despite Bond's popularity slump, Nintendo and Rare attempted to build hype. The rest of the world found out about Rare and *GoldenEye* in January 1995, when a British paper ran an article about how Rare had "beat the rest of the world for the rights to make the new James Bond game." An April *Nintendo Power* article boosted the announcement with photos of Tim Stamper visiting Leavesden to meet with the film's art director and production designers. From its earliest stages, Nintendo's publicity around the game focused on how closely tied to the movie it would be.

The *Nintendo Power* article also implied that *GoldenEye* would be a Super Nintendo game—a side-scrolling platformer like *Robocop* with the 3D rendered graphics Rare had made famous in *Killer Instinct* and *Donkey Kong Country*: one newspaper article previewing the game was even titled "Donkey Bond." But Martin Hollis refused to make the game on anything other than the N64, so the SNES idea was dropped.

In the original contract for the project, Rare intended to release *GoldenEye* close to the film's release, by Christmas 1995. "It was supposed to be a three-person project and take nine months or something," Hollis said later. "No one told me it would take three years […] ten people [and $2 million] because no one knew."

•

More and more people slowly filled up the conference room as Duncan Botwood, a wildly talented architecture school dropout and RPG fan with a rich imagination, showed off his art portfolio. The pages spread out on the table included technical architecture drawings in pen and watercolors, CAD (computer-aided design and drafting) mock-ups, as well as a smaller manila folder full of world concepts Botwood had dreamed up while working boring temp jobs. As he waited for diners to finish eating at a hotel or rode the bus out to read a gas meter, Botwood scribbled down ideas like a re-imagining of the radio hit *The Shadow* as an all-bird universe that he called "The Sparrow." One of Botwood's worlds featured a skull in a jar who could slot into different vehicles and tools and operate them. Another starred a magnetic robot who bounced around by reversing his polarities.

Rare production manager Simon Farmer, who was running the interview, had brought in several other staff, including Martin Hollis, to sit around the long table and look at Botwood's work.

"What would you make for a James Bond game?" one of them asked.

"How long do you have?" Botwood answered. Not only had he read all the Fleming novels and seen all the films, but owned the sourcebook for a James Bond tabletop RPG that a friend from college had photocopied for him and put into a three-ring binder. The Rare staffers listened eagerly as Botwood rattled off ideas about gadgets, cars, and guns, though he wasn't sure why they kept asking about Bond. When he left the interview that day, Botwood had no idea if he would land the job. He ended up with a starting salary offer higher than those of his friends graduating from architecture programs.

Botwood was one of the seven people that Hollis hand-selected for the *GoldenEye* team, picking them up one at a time as the project went on. Hollis took the task of assembling his team seriously. "Of course I wanted good people, enthusiastic about the Bond universe," he said years later, "though not all of them were. They were just incredibly good craftspeople. I actually made a list of everyone in the company involved with development and scored them out of ten. I wrote notes on the side, too, and I spoke to Simon Farmer in production about each one and he'd tell me, 'Oh, you don't want them…' He knew if they were suitable for the project." When a reporter in 2018 asked if he felt like Bond's boss M putting together a dossier on everyone at Rare, Hollis teased "Well, I did wear all black at the time and had a confident swagger." Although Hollis's team were all excellent artists and programmers, almost all of them were game design rookies.

As newbies, the developers had no egos back then, but even after all their wild successes, they still have no egos now. I've found, for instance, that if you try to compliment one of the *GoldenEye* developers on their game, they usually respond with one of three moves: deflect your compliment onto the rest of the team; deny your compliment and insist that the game wasn't as good as you remember it; or express profound gratitude that they got to help make it. ("I'm just a normal bloke, so it's nice to be asked about anything," one of them told me.) Some of them literally flinched when I tried to praise them.

Mark Edmonds, *GoldenEye*'s first programmer and the first team member to join Hollis in the *GoldenEye* project, exemplifies the team's profound humility. He has curly brown hair, big glasses, and a soft-spoken, shy way about him—unless, of course, you ask him about something technical; the man lights up when he talks about code, and even emailed me some of the actual game code after our interview. Behind him during our Zoom call loomed a massive bookshelf full of sci-fi and fantasy books; he especially loves Peter F. Hamilton's massive space operas. Edmonds's humble demeanor belies a man who several other members of the team called "an absolute genius" who "would win the coding Olympics."

Edmonds grew up surrounded by computers: His father sold them for IBM. From an early age, he dreamed of making games like the ones he played on his ZX Spectrum and Atari 2600. His school didn't offer any computer courses, so he had to teach himself how to program. He studied mathematics in college and read all the programming books he could get his hands on to prepare himself for a career in the games industry. But he couldn't find a job in the field after graduation, so he worked for three years with a medical programming company and built up his experience. When he started looking for games jobs again, he found an ad for Rare in *Edge* advertising the "Ultra 64" project. The company's cutting-edge technology and relationship with Nintendo excited Edmonds—"plus, they were in the countryside," he told me, and the drive to Twycross for his interview, lined with flowers all along the way, "made such a good impression."

Edmonds, employee number 35, started at Rare in early January 1995. His first task on the job? A full day of playing *Ridge Racer* on the PlayStation, followed by a month of training spent working on an odd project for Hollis. "I didn't really know what I was working on," Edmonds said in 2018. "I was asked to investigate creating filleted ["angled"] joints for an animated 3D character system; basically, a smooth skin over joints, like an elbow, rather than just having a solid block for an upper and lower arm. I had no idea it was connected to James Bond but I must have passed the test because I got moved [...] onto the team proper. It was great just to be working on my first video game!"

•

A curvy, bright red Ferrari graced the screen of new Rare artist Karl Hilton's computer—a 3D model he'd been building for several weeks to teach himself Rare's software. A car nut himself, Hilton hadn't believed his ears when his bosses had suggested he model the car as an orientation project. "You've got to be kidding me," he'd thought. He already felt like he was working his dream job, but it was about to get even better.

A tall, lean man dressed in all black, his long hair tied back in a ponytail, popped his head into Hilton's office. "Do you like James Bond?" he asked.

Hilton had seen Martin Hollis around the Rare campus, but had never formally met him before. While Hollis worked in a suite of offices with the *Killer Instinct* team, Hilton had spent his first few months at Rare in a training room in a separate building.

"I love James Bond," Hilton answered, without hesitation.

"Okay, well, I'm putting together a team to make a James Bond game and I need an environmental artist," Hollis said. "Are you interested?"

"Absolutely I'm interested," Hilton answered, and just like that, he became the first artist to join the Bond team.

Hilton was a trained architect with a deep passion for games. Like Edmonds, Hilton grew up playing anything he could get his hands on. And, like Hollis, as soon as he got a computer, he started making his own games and sending them off to computer magazines that published the code of reader-submitted games. One of these published games even came with a £100 prize, which felt like a fortune to him as a boy. In college, Hilton developed another passion: CAD architecture. He would wait outside his school's CAD lab every morning at 7 a.m. just so he could snag a spot on one of its Macintoshes and work there all day long. He even used to take school computers home with him over the holidays. "I remember my dad complaining about the electricity," Hilton told me, "because I had all these computers humming away in my bedroom rendering stuff all the time. I had to move out of my bedroom because I couldn't sleep because of the noise." He went on to study computer visualization animation in Bournemouth University's master's program—the only one of its kind in the country at the time—and started at Rare shortly after. "I got to go make video games, which I had always wanted to and tried to do as a kid, but I didn't think anybody was ever going to pay me to do it," he told me.

Although he felt excited about joining the Bond team, in the back of his mind, Hilton also worried. "I was thinking, 'Oh God, a film license,'" he said in 2011, citing "generally awful" other licensed games from the era like 1993's *Robocop 3*. "It seemed a risky project." He also, like Edmonds, had never worked professionally on a game with a team. "We were all very, very equally inexperienced," Hilton told me. "We were all pretty much fresh out of university."

Brett Jones, a second artist assigned to the project just after Hilton, was another recent university hire. Jones was the goofy jokester on the team who always found ways to lighten the mood, like giving everyone nicknames. (He called Edmonds, who is very tall, "The Length".) Our Zoom interview turned into a brief tour of Jones's house—he showed me some of his Star Trek memorabilia and the movie theatre-sized posters of the Pierce Brosnan Bond films—including *GoldenEye*, of course—hanging in his hallway. "Like any self-respecting nerd, I have tons of things," he told me. Jones is truly a collector at heart—he still has all the art he made as a child, all his references from college art classes, and all of his notes and sketches from the *GoldenEye* development period, which he was kind enough to share with me. Jones's collecting influence played a crucial role in *GoldenEye*'s development since he supplied many of the team's artistic reference material from his own personal collection of Bond books and memorabilia. You see Jones's collecting impulse every time you select your multiplayer character out of the game's 33 different choices, since Jones designed all the character models.

Jones studied graphic design in college and attended the same master's program in computer animation and visualization as Hilton—the two actually sat next to each other in one class, where they instantly bonded over Star Trek. After graduation, Jones applied to a job at Rare upon Hilton's recommendation, and stayed with him the night before the interview.

"What do I need to tell them?" Jones asked Hilton. The problem was that Jones knew nothing about video games and had rarely played any before.

"Talk about *Virtua Cop* [a hot arcade shooter at the time] and how much you love playing it," Hilton advised. When Jones repeated what Hilton had rehearsed with him, he got the job before the end of the interview.

Jones spent his first three months at Rare alone in a room reading books and watching videotapes to teach himself Alias Wavefront (later renamed "Maya")—a 3D modeling package used to make sprites. Although he found it a bit of a lonely introduction to work, Jones taught himself how to model, rig, light, animate, and render during those three months, building starships from Star Trek for practice the same way Hilton had built Ferraris. At some point, Hollis and Edmonds asked Jones to build a character model so they could have something to test in the game engine. Looking back, Jones says, "[the model] was awful. He was too tall, he was too spindly, he was too thin, but at the time I was very, very pleased with it." Hollis seemed pleased, too, because shortly after, he invited Jones to join the Bond team full time.

The last person to join the team in these earliest days was Duncan Botwood, the imaginative creator of sparrow worlds who started at Rare in March 1995, shortly after Jones. Botwood is a creative, funny soul who loves to bake—his Twitter feed is full of photos of his newest creations, from rhubarb crumbles to mince pies. Botwood grew up playing ColecoVision and ZX Spectrum—he still shudders at his memory of the keyboard's "rubbery dead flesh" feeling. He loved escaping into fantasy and sci-fi worlds in video games and tabletop RPG games, and he doodled constantly, making up his own worlds like the ones he would later show in his Rare interview. Botwood dropped out after two years of architecture school because the courses focused more on the technical elements of the profession than the artistic side that he loved. Still, he took away a lot from architecture school about the flow of spaces and how people engage in them—skills that would serve him well as a creator of level spaces in *GoldenEye*.

For the members of the Bond team, starting at Rare in the mid-90s as a young, inexperienced game developer felt a bit like hitting the jackpot. "I turned up there from university, [Rare had] finished *Donkey*

Kong Country, and I remember hearing they'd all got paid bonuses of thousands of pounds, which as an impoverished student sounded incredible," Hilton told Eurogamer. "They'd all been taken to somewhere nice on holiday as well for a week—taken off to some Caribbean island to say thank you for the work. So you felt like you had landed in this paradise where you were being paid to make video games [...] So it was like, right. This is my chance here, so I had better get on with it." All eyes were on the rookies now—it was time for the young developers to prove what they could do.

A VIEW TO A GAME

THE MOST INFLUENTIAL CONSOLE first-person shooter of all time began as a list of questions on an unassuming scrap of paper. As he assembled his team, Martin Hollis, ever the curious type, began *GoldenEye*'s development process by writing up some early "questions important to bond game," which included: "What is the appropriate level of Humour? What is the appropriate level of Violence? Can we get footage as soon as it is shot? Can we use actual music? Music from which films? Can we use [the] title sequence and music? Can we use [the] likeness of good and bad guys and gals? Can we use likenesses/material/episodes from other Bond films?"

The answers to these questions would eventually become some of *GoldenEye*'s key defining features: the perfect balance of humor, violence, and humorous violence; the extensive references to *GoldenEye* the movie and its characters (as well as other Bond movies and their characters); and the iconic music and title sequence from the film series. At the bottom of these early notes, Hollis included a list of "photos of props" he hoped to get from the movie studio. When Hollis shared this initial wish list with Nintendo, they responded with an "extremely detailed document" explaining everything he could use in the game, which turned out to be "an astonishing amount," Hollis said later. "We were very lucky to have such a broad license."

Hollis's *GoldenEye* game design document reveals ambitious, innovative ideas helpfully rooted in a clear model: *Virtua Cop*, a 1994 first-person-shooter Sega arcade game in which players used a light gun to shoot bad guys popping out from behind obstacles. The game sent players on a pre-scripted, set path from which they couldn't diverge—a genre called a "rail shooter" for how it kept players "on rails." With *GoldenEye,* Hollis basically wanted to take *Virtua Cop* and make it bigger. He proposed fast-paced, action-packed missions to avoid monotonous and repetitive gameplay; a highly interactive game environment where players could blow up everything in sight; and extensive visual effects ranging from muzzle flashes to bullet holes in the walls. The gameplay would be on rails like *Virtua Cop*, but *GoldenEye* would have more character types, more animations, more intelligent AI, more interactive objects, and more interesting 3D backgrounds. In other words, more of everything. The document proposed that Bond would complete missions based on the film plot but also expanding on that plot, varying between "covert, sabotage, clandestine, and rescue missions," many of which would require Bond to stay stealthy and quiet.

Though Hollis was excited to tap into the N64's vast potential and Rare's boundless resources, he also felt the pressure of the project from the beginning. One of the first problems the team encountered was that when they started work on the game, they had no access to the N64's hardware: no development systems, final specs, or controller—only emulators for the N64 chipset. And so they went into the first year of the design process totally uninformed, with Edmonds and Hollis focused on programming the engine, Hilton on level architecture, Jones on character models, and Botwood on a bit of everything.

It took a year to get *GoldenEye*'s game engine up and running. At most studios today, an entire company shares an engine—the basic technical framework for how the game runs—but at Rare during the *GoldenEye* years, every team wrote their own engine from scratch, ultra-optimized for their project and with no superfluous elements. Essentially, then, the team spent the initial third of *GoldenEye*'s development process making tools to make the game before they could start making the game—like a film director building his own lights and cameras. "We were just making it up as we went along," Edmonds told me. "It's just so completely different from the Unreal or Unity engine today, [which] basically just do everything for you."

Hollis and Edmonds's first technical challenge was building a pipeline to move the graphics from the artists' design software into the N64. "I spent a lot of time working on this kind of thing all throughout the project," Edmonds told me, collaborating closely with the artists to make them exactly the tools they needed. Hilton would request a piece of software and the programmers would write it for him and add any tweaks he needed.

"I was technical enough that I could talk to them in programmer language about what I wanted and needed to do and why I wanted to do it that way," Hilton told me, "and they were interested in the art enough to really want to enable that." The programmers' work was nothing short of miraculous. All the two had to guide them was a bit of very basic software and documents from Nintendo, but for the most part, they had to consult textbooks for help as they invented techniques out of thin air.

They next built a rail shooter game engine with a spline through the world that the camera would move along. Hollis wrote the code for hit-testing and Edmonds tinkered with it, then added simple cuboid hitbox testing on props and character limbs. "The hit-test and detection-work probably came about as we originally started making the game in the style of the arcade games *Virtua Cop* (1994) and *Time Crisis* (1995), where aiming and hitting the right thing was a crucial part of the gameplay," Edmonds said in 2018. The team members spent a lot of time and money playing their model game *Virtua Cop* at the local Sega World arcade; Jones still remembers Hollis feeding the machine 50-pence coins until they'd played through the whole game.

Although *Virtua Cop* was a practical model, since an on-rails shooter would be easier to make, Hollis had always wanted to make a truly open, "free movement" 3D first-person shooter, and his game design document hedged its bets. On page 2, in a section called "Control," he noted that movement may be automatic, fixed, or under player control. "At this point the team was happy to contemplate making two modes for the game, an on-rails mode and [an] FPS mode," Hollis explained in 2004. "[W]e didn't know what the control of the N64 would be like, so it made designing the control system difficult at such an early stage. We didn't have any N64s, or anything like them." In the end, the team would have to wait until they could see what the N64 was capable of before they could make any final decisions about gameplay and controls.

•

The Bond team was as baffled as they were dazzled. Spread in front of them was the most glorious chef-prepared buffet they'd ever seen, but they couldn't figure out where to pay for their plates. "It's all free," their fixer explained, which left them even more astounded. On fancy film sets like this one—the set of *GoldenEye* the movie—the food was always free.

The young men settled at a table and Botwood excused himself to use the restroom. Jones showed his friends a quick glimpse of his pocket's contents: shell casings and exploded fake glass he'd plucked off the ground of the runway set as souvenirs. As the others ogled Jones's souvenirs, someone suddenly started whispering excitedly and the air in the room shifted—Pierce Brosnan had just entered the studio canteen for lunch. He disappeared as soon as he had arrived, though, and Botwood, upon his return from the restroom, caught only a brief glance of the back of James Bond's head.

Although they had longer to wait on the N64, the team got early access to all the elements of the *GoldenEye* film and were even driven, in the backseat of a Mercedes, down to the film studio two hours south in Leavesden during shooting. As the team was chaperoned around the sets, Hilton and Jones took photographs of everything they could see, "from props and costumes to all of the actual film sets and even models and miniatures," Hilton told MEL Magazine. "I took hundreds of photos on 35mm film—we used them as reference for all of the in-game art." Jones also lugged along a heavy, expensive digital camera—one of the first available—to capture reference material. They even took VHS video of one set visit, including footage of Edmonds exploring the film's archives set and Hilton posing by a Tiger helicopter.

"Everything you see in the game is as close as we could get" to the film original, Jones told me. Some in-game textures are actual photographs from the set visit, fed directly from the digital camera to the artists' software, then scaled down. This allowed all the characters, props, and level environments to match the movie set exactly, right down to the Russian words on walls and barrels or the evil character Boris's—in Jones's words—"ghastly" bold patterned shirt. All these carefully replicated textures and models from the movie set resulted in a game that closely matched the aesthetic of the film.

They also made for a stunningly realistic gaming experience at a time when most first-person shooters took place in sci-fi labyrinths or cartoonish dungeons. *GoldenEye* was the first game ever to recreate real-world film sets this meticulously, and since the movie's locations, costumes, and props were modeled on real guns, military uniforms, and locations in Cuba and Russia, the game felt uniquely realistic for its era. "No one had tried to create ultra-realistic environments before," an anonymous team member said in 2001, "simply because they hadn't had enough reason to. *GoldenEye* was the perfect opportunity, and I'd hate to think of the lengths you'd have to go to repeat the effort if there wasn't a film being made at the time."

•

The beginning of *GoldenEye*'s Facility mission may be one of the most iconic of any game level. You find yourself crawling through the vents of an enemy chemical weapons facility to an entry duct in the restroom ceiling. If you aim just right, you can murder an unsuspecting guard minding his own business in one of the toilet stalls, then drop down into your own stall, bust out the door and kill the guard standing at the sink. The toilet stall level entrance is a classic gaming moment that signifies the start of a whole new era of stealth-oriented gameplay. And it wouldn't have been possible without the genius work of Karl Hilton, the *GoldenEye* team's lead environmental artist.

The first step in Hilton's level creation process involved planning out which locations the game would explore, based around the plot of *GoldenEye* the movie. The film follows Bond as he attempts to prevent his old friend and ex-MI6 agent 006 Alec Trevelyan from turning a dangerous satellite called GoldenEye on London and unleashing global financial chaos. Assisting Bond is Russian computer programmer Natalya Simonova, who operates in the game as both ally and damsel constantly needing rescuing. In addition to Trevelyan, the film and game featured additional baddies like evil General Arkady Ourumov, hacker Boris Grishenko, and dominatrix Xenia Onatopp (yes, that is really her name and yes, she did in fact murder a character in the film by squeezing him to death with her thighs during sex).

GoldenEye the game follows the movie's plot pretty precisely, with the first three levels recreating the film's opening sequence and the rest following Bond as he sneaks around Russian bases, finding clues as to Trevelyan's identity and secret plans, then unmasks and pursues Trevelyan across St. Petersburg to a final confrontation at the GoldenEye satellite's radio antenna dish in the jungles of Cuba. But the game's plot also expands on the film and offers players even more to do than what they had seen on the movie screen. Hollis wanted a healthy number of levels in the game but felt the film didn't have enough material to make that happen, so the team padded out the story with extra missions that extend beyond the movie, or missions that place Bond in the movie's cool setpieces even if they hadn't involved him in the actual film.

"When we had plenty of film material, we tried to stick to it for authenticity but we weren't afraid of adding to it to help the game design," Hilton explained later. "It was very organic."

In this way, the game holds on to the visual spectacle so central to Bond films while acknowledging that games are a different medium than films. "By sticking too close to the film, there's a risk of becoming too didactic, even too pedantic in the sequencing," Hollis has explained.

These additional levels—like Surface, Dam, and Silo—allowed Hilton more freedom since they didn't need to recreate anything from the film. Dam, for instance, came about after a team member suggested they let the player spend more time infiltrating the base leading up to the famous bungee jump that kicks off the film. The subterranean Caverns level, Botwood's idea, was inspired by the question: "Where does all the water from the satellite control base in the Control level go?"

and served as a nice way to move the player from the Jungle level into Control.

"If it wasn't in the movie, then I didn't have to worry about it looking like the movie," Hilton noted, so he could design these levels for peak technical performance, with less advanced textures to ensure a faster frame rate.

For levels that did recreate scenes from the movie, Hilton achieved a high degree of verisimilitude thanks to photos taken on location as well as scripts and set blueprints provided by the movie studio. Bringing each location to life was largely Hilton's and Botwood's responsibility, with a few other levels designed by Jones and Ady Smith, a lead environmental artist and visual effects artist who joined the team later.

The artists started by creating wireframe models of each level location, then texture-mapped those models by wrapping a photograph around the 3D wire skeleton. "Initially what I did was I looked at the plans that we had from the movie sets," Hilton told me, "but that was never ever remotely usable as a game design. So at that point I would start to build out extra bits that added action." For instance, he would add in extra rooms he imagined the Russian bad guys would need in their base. "I would tend to use gridded papers and draw out a plan," Hilton said, and then he would model it and later make changes based on gameplay needs. "It was very quick," he said. "I could do that in an afternoon and then we could play it again and then see whether it worked or not."

The first level the team made was Bunker, a Russian base consisting of labyrinthine tiled hallways, big steel doors, and ominous security cameras. According to Botwood, Hilton made Bunker as a kind of test bed for tinkering purposes. "We put a spline through the level so you could follow a route like in *Virtua Cop*, but it didn't go further than that," Hilton told *Now Gamer*. "Some of those early builds had bits missing because you'd never be able to see them and I remember going back [after the game came off the rails] and filling in the holes."

Statue Park, a cemetery of old Soviet statues and the setting of Trevelyan's climactic unmasking, was Jones's special project, and he worked hard to make the space look exactly like what he'd seen on set. The original film set, it turns out, was inspired by real-life Moscow open-air museums such as Memento Park in Budapest and Fallen Monument Park in Moscow, where Soviet symbols were tucked away after the fall of Communism. The level, then, may be responsible for teaching a generation of twelve-year-olds who Lenin was, thanks to a mission objective that required you to meet Trevelyan at a statue of Lenin.

Jones did acknowledge to me that he accidentally put a confusing misdirection into the space: seven giant statues of the letter "C" in seven different locations in the level that often end up misdirecting the player. "I thought, 'Let's put some more of those cool letters and some of those big statues that I took photos of,' because

I wanted to make it look just like the Statue Park that we had seen," Jones told me. "I wasn't thinking that if you put [a C] in here and [a C] in there, people will get confused and they won't know where they are."

Jones also worked on the Jungle location with Smith, who was assigned to the level since he had experience and skill making pre-rendered jungle foliage on *Donkey Kong Country*. Smith and Jones had to rely on fog to give the N64 a bit of a break from rendering all the polygons and colors on Jungle's plants and trees—a move they felt self-conscious about since they didn't want to recreate the "pea soup" gaming experience that had defined *Turok: Dinosaur Hunter* (1997). On the other hand, though, the fog fits perfectly for the misty jungle, and makes the scope on the level's assault rifle even more fun to use.

The constraint of the film's plot forced the team to attempt "insane" levels like Cradle, the game's very last level, which takes place (in accordance with the film) on top of the satellite control antenna, and Streets, which recreated an important chase scene through the streets of St. Petersburg from the film. Both levels posed enormous technical challenges, but in the end, "[i]f we'd gone for levels that were easier for us to do, *GoldenEye* may not have been so good," an anonymous team member later said.

The Streets level was made using grid-like blocks, Botwood told me, and he also pointed out a mistake at the end of the level, which was originally supposed to feature a gate with a big star on it leading into the Depot level's railway yard. "I think I forgot in the final version to submit the version that had the gate in," Botwood told me. "I think we were all waiting for the asset and I might have put it in and then not saved it." Indeed, if you watch the cutscene at the end of the level, you'll see a gray cloud where the gate should be.

Even still, Hilton and Botwood's attention to detail in their level designs and textures was impeccable. Hilton used source texts like Soviet propaganda posters and, for the Aztec temple level, a coffee table book containing ancient artwork. The team put "everything in it that you shouldn't do in a 3D game," Hilton joked just after the game's release.

Sometimes Hilton's details were meant purely to add humor, in the form of Easter eggs and little inside jokes. A chemistry set placed inexplicably in the rafters of the Facility's ceiling, for instance, was "put in the game because we always appreciate seeing little details like this in other games," an anonymous team member later said. Other silly little touches include: a red "no" sign imposed over a silhouetted image of Bond that appears above a door in the Facility level; the Rare logo graffitied on a wall in the Depot level; and a VHS copy of *GoldenEye* the movie in the Bunker level.

Not all of Hilton's inside jokes made it into the final game, however. "One of Nintendo's eagle-eyed polyglot testers spotted the Russian word for 'vodka' on crates in the game," Hollis told me, "despite one or two individuals on the Bond team having confidence that they would not. Nintendo insisted we change the texture. Nintendo is strictly a family-friendly firm and that doesn't include families that drink vodka." The crates in the final version say "vadko."

One of the most common Easter eggs, which did manage to survive every round of testing, is Hilton's own name. "Karl" and "K.H." show up in Depot graffiti, and "KH-89" and "K.I.H." show up in the missile Silo level and others. "It annoyed the programmers a lot," Hilton told me, laughing, "because it was hard for them to do that kind of thing. They were doing all this work on the code and then they'd run around the level and there was my name." Although they were creating one of the most influential video games in history, Hilton pointed out to me, the Bond team didn't know that at the time. They were still the rookies at Rare, after all, and they thought management had just given them a cast-off practice assignment, so they put weird little things into the game without a single thought that people would still be looking this closely at their work 25 years later.

YOU KNOW THE NAME.
YOU KNOW THE NUMBER.

IN NOVEMBER 1995, *GoldenEye,* the seventeenth Bond film in the series, premiered at Radio City Music Hall in New York. Paparazzi and news media lined the red carpet, and even Pierce Brosnan, glamorous girlfriend on his arm, seemed a little overwhelmed about making his debut as the new James Bond.

Would Brosnan make a better Bond than Timothy Dalton? The world was eager to find out. Brosnan was 42 at the start of his Bond career, with a ton of pressure riding on him: "Connery, Moore, Dalton, even one-shot wonder George Lazenby—they had it easy," a reporter wrote at the time. "All they had to do was save the world. Brosnan has to save the franchise."

GoldenEye's producers hoped a new Bond actor would reinvigorate the struggling franchise. The studio had already wanted Brosnan to take over the role of Bond back in 1986, but he couldn't get out of his contract for the TV show *Remington Steele*, and so Dalton stepped into his wildly unpopular turn at the role instead. Interestingly, the opening of *GoldenEye* the film takes place nine years in the past, which would have been 1986. "It is almost as if the film is turning the clock back to suggest that Brosnan should really have been Bond all along, that Dalton had been an aberration," one Bond scholar wrote.

The first time viewers saw Brosnan's face in the role of Bond on screen was upside-down in a bathroom stall—the iconic film scene that inspired the opening to the game's Facility mission. Director Martin Campbell had wanted to introduce Bond in a more playful, humorous way, and was ultimately shocked that the producers allowed it. But this reflected the kind of Bond Brosnan was: lighter and more relaxed than the intensely serious Dalton; witty, intelligent, and sneaky as opposed to his successor Daniel Craig's grittier, more muscular Bond. Brosnan's Bond was very British: handsome, debonair, clean, and formal, and also, in film critic Roger Ebert's words, "more sensitive, more vulnerable, more psychologically complete" than previous Bonds.

Every fan has their own Bond, and mine is Brosnan. When I close my eyes and picture James Bond, Pierce Brosnan's face—not Sean Connery's or Daniel Craig's—pops into my mind. In every way, Brosnan was a "Bond of the Millennium," as Bond expert Nicolás Suszczyk calls him—the Bond of a changing time. *GoldenEye* featured a new director, new writers, new producers, and new actors playing Bond, M, and Moneypenny; it was the first Bond film to use CGI, the first to come out on DVD, and the first not based on an Ian Fleming novel.

GoldenEye was also the first Bond movie released after the end of the Cold War. The Berlin Wall had fallen and old enemies had become new allies. The Soviet Union no longer existed and communism—Bond's age-old enemy since his beginnings—no longer felt like a global threat (although that didn't stop the film from making Russians the bad guys—old clichés die hard). "It's a new world," declared one ad from the era, "with new enemies and new threats… but you can still depend on one man… 007."

Thematically, *GoldenEye* the film and the game are very much about the passage of time—about how Bond responds to social and political changes in the world around him. The movie's opening flashback to a Soviet chemical weapons facility nine years ago—an unusual move for a Bond film, which usually operate firmly in the present—emphasizes the different world of 1995 while connecting the series to its past. The opening credit sequence that follows the flashback—in which beautiful silhouetted women stand on crumbled statues of Lenin and hammers and sickles—symbolizes the triumphalist way the West thought of Russia at the time, and was so offensive in some Communist territories at the time that the film was actually censored there.

Bond films have always looked out to the world to make themselves culturally relevant, and are therefore in turn always a commentary on an era's popular culture. In the 1990s and 2000s, when people increasingly feared the growing influence of technology (Y2K, anyone?),

Brosnan's Bond exceled with gadgets—a fact very much reflected in the game adaptation. Brosnan's Bond was more technological than Dalton's or Craig's Bonds, and in *GoldenEye*, the bad guys weaponize information and surveillance technology, like Trevelyan's satellite or his security cameras in the bunker. It's no accident that you spend so much time in the game blowing up cameras and computers, the new enemies of the era.

On the flipside, technical knowledge—like Natalya's computer expertise and the datathiefs and covert modems Bond uses to steal information in the game—proved particularly powerful in 1995. In this way, *GoldenEye* addressed concerns like, according to academic Martin Willis: "What place is there for the human in an increasingly technological world? What power will technology wield in the future? What impact will global information and communication networks have on the continued prosperity of the nation-state?" Bond's bungee leap off the dam at the start of the film and game might as well be him diving into the unknown modern world. This tech dive persists until, in the final Brosnan film, Bond drives an invisible car like a superhero.

Perhaps nothing captures *GoldenEye*'s themes of change better than Mike Myers's 1997 comedy *Austin Powers: International Man of Mystery*, which was as much a spoof on *GoldenEye* in particular as it was on the Bond franchise as a whole. In the movie, Bond caricature Austin Powers, a top British spy utterly irresistible to women, is cryogenically frozen in the 1960s and thawed in the 1990s. When he wakes up, his new colleague Vanessa must acclimate him to the 90s, which starts with a lesson in workplace sexual harassment.

This running gag throughout Austin Powers—that Austin's flirtatious banter around women is his greatest weakness—reflects a huge conversation about *GoldenEye* in the mid-90s. At one point early in the film, Judi Dench, in her first scene ever as the new M, calls Bond a "misogynistic dinosaur." Anxiety about how this dinosaur could hold up against his new foe—the politically correct 90s—pervaded critics' writings at the time, with a mention in almost every review and news story about the film.

Casting a woman as M was a conscious choice by director Martin Campbell, and publicity for the film touted Bond girls who were less subservient and more independent than in the past. Natalya, Bond's main love interest in the film and game, is an adept computer programmer who even takes out guards with a Cougar Magnum in the game. "Gone are the bimbos!" touted one press release, and Famke Janssen, the actress who played the film's fighter pilot femme fatale Xenia Onatopp, was indeed so hardcore that she actually sent another actor to the hospital during production—an anecdote that turned into its own kind of publicity for the film's badass women. "What can I say?" she said at the time. "I got carried away."

But even with these changes, Bond remained stubbornly sexist, and intentionally so. "We've got a female

M, we've got stronger women, we've got better acting, and Bond still remains as politically incorrect as he always did," Campbell said during filming. No one was a louder defender of Bond's sexism than Brosnan, who proudly announced in interviews at the time that Bond is a "man's man"—a "chauvinist" who will punch any woman who "misbehaves."

Despite—or, sadly, perhaps because of—the sexism, Brosnan and *GoldenEye* managed to make Bond relevant again after the character's long absence and popularity slump. *GoldenEye* hit it big at the box office, with the UK's highest non-holiday opening in history at the time and the third-best opening ever, just behind *Jurassic Park* and *Batman Forever*. *GoldenEye* had the biggest opening of any previous Bond film and the biggest of any in MGM history. Worldwide, the film grossed more than *The Living Daylights* and *License to Kill* combined, at $356 million, making it the most successful Bond film since *Moonraker* in 1979. As for the critics, they all agreed that *GoldenEye* breathed new life into the franchise and that Brosnan played the best Bond since Connery. *GoldenEye* still often ranks in the top ten best Bond films and forever bears the distinction of being the movie that saved James Bond.

•

That same November, across the world at the Shoshinkai video-game trade show hosted by Nintendo just outside

Tokyo, a different *GoldenEye* made its debut. The first day of the trade show, throngs of schoolkids anxiously lined up in the cold outside the convention hall just for a chance to lay eyes, for the very first time, on the much-anticipated (and still unfinished) Nintendo 64 console and its incredible, intensely hyped 3D games, including *GoldenEye*.

Unlike *GoldenEye* the film, *GoldenEye* the game premiered not in its final, polished form but as a very rough teaser for what still lay ahead. The early promotional video of the game that aired at Shoshinkai in 1995 featured footage from the Archives level. In that footage, all the art—the cardboard boxes lining the corridors, the colors on the walls, and the railings on the stairs—looked the same as in the final version of the level. But the gameplay didn't look anything like the final version, where players run the halls of the large building hunting for Natalya and the helicopter black box. In the Shoshinkai footage, the player's movement was still on rails, slow and pre-scripted, and no gun even appeared on screen. Guards in green uniforms simply died on cue, with no shots fired. "The Shoshinkai on-rails shooter footage was not interactive, or was only 25% interactive," Hollis told me. "Really it was a sham or a facade, as so much footage at trade shows is."

The game engine still wasn't complete, let alone missions or objectives. But now that the game's film namesake had debuted, the Rare team had missed its first in-house deadline, and the *GoldenEye* name became less and less relevant every day. "At no time did I think,

'They've released the film, maybe we should have released the game at this point,'" Jones said later, "because it wasn't even anywhere close."

"The original idea was there would be a glittering launch simultaneously with [the N64], which would be synchronised with the release of the *GoldenEye* movie," Hollis later said, but by November 1995, both the N64 and the game had fallen far behind this schedule. Since the N64 was still a long way off from finished, the possibility remained that *GoldenEye* could debut with the N64 as a launch title. But the team would need to expand again to aim for such a goal.

•

Martin Hollis was confused by a fax he'd found in the Rare company fax machine, addressed to his colleague David Doak and advertising a job in New Zealand. Doak had only been at Rare for about six months, and the company had extremely low turnover because employees got so invested in their games. But that was just the problem—as a systems administrator, Doak got to visit all the different offices at Rare and catch glimpses of all the fun games in-progress—but he couldn't work on anything himself. Six months of this torture had made Doak antsy. He felt like the IT guy in Willy Wonka's chocolate factory.

"Why wouldn't you want to stay here?" Hollis asked Doak, handing him the fax.

"I'd like to help make the games here, but I'm not a programmer," Doak replied.

"Well, I'd like you to be on the *GoldenEye* team," Hollis responded. "You can pick up some coding and I'm sure there's some stuff you can do that's design or coding-based."

Hollis's offer was bold, considering Doak had no formal programming experience. But it persuaded Doak to stay at Rare, and also set the course for the direction of *GoldenEye*.

"After the first year, and we missed our first deadline, management started to get very concerned, and gave us more people," Hollis said in 2004. "I guess it was either that or cancel the project, and the work we had to show was impressive enough not to cancel."

25 years after the game's debut, Doak is the human mascot of *GoldenEye*—he's constantly giving interviews, consulting with modders, joking around with fans, and retweeting *GoldenEye* memes. He's also responsible, along with Botwood, for *GoldenEye*'s objectives, object placement, and its cheeky mission briefings.

Doak is outgoing—during our Zoom call, he laughed easily at my worst jokes. With his polo shirts, neat beard, and long gray hair tied back in a ponytail, he looks like an exceptionally cool scientist, which is exactly what he is—a biochemist, to be precise. Doak grew up in Belfast eagerly awaiting each year's new Bond movie and staying up all night playing video games with his brother. He went on to spend ten years at Oxford earning his BA, MA, and PhD in biochemistry and then staying for a post-doc. In other words, he earned his role as "Dr. Doak" in *GoldenEye*. Before *GoldenEye*, he published papers with titles like "High Resolution H NMR study of the solution structure of the S4 segment of the sodium channel protein." Most importantly, Doak's research on modeling protein structures gave him experience using powerful, expensive Silicon Graphics computers.

One day in 1995, as Doak flipped through an issue of *Edge* at the office, he stumbled across a job ad from Rare seeking a system manager for their network of Silicon Graphics machines. Doak knew Rare well from his youth playing Ultimate's ZX Spectrum games, so he applied "for a laugh," assuming he had limited chances of getting the job. But at the time, SG workstations were so expensive and rare that Doak was one of the few people in the UK who could operate one. Doak had "inadvertently […] acquired a skill which was in high demand in the video game sector at that time," he said later, so he nabbed the Rare job easily. And then, after ten years training as a biochemist, Doak left it all to, as he explained it to his shocked mother, "run away with the circus"—a choice he's never regretted.

When Doak first started at Rare, his sole job was to take care of refrigerator-sized SG machines with sci-fi nicknames like "The Death Star," some of which cost up to a million pounds. (One artist later tweeted that "when I was working on *GoldenEye* I was working on a machine that cost more than my house.") Despite the high cost, "it was an incredibly brittle machine," Doak said later. "It used to crash all the time." Hollis sometimes had to reboot the SG machine "Challenger" multiple times a day, and at one point, Edmonds told me, Hilton's machine got so overheated it caught on fire.

After Doak joined the Bond team, he continued working as systems administrator while teaching himself to code. To learn the basics, he started by programming the game's pause menu, which was designed to look like Bond's fancy gadget watch. When you pause *GoldenEye*, your first-person viewpoint shifts down to Bond's wrist and the watch interface fills the screen, displaying the status of mission objectives, a list of weapons and gadgets, and controller setting options. It also really does tell time—in-game time, at least. The watch time on the evening mission Statue, for instance, reads 8:10, whereas the sunnier daylight Frigate level takes place at 2:35.

As detail-oriented as these touches are, Doak acknowledges that the watch menu does have one weird feature: when you press pause, the game doesn't immediately pause but rather begins an animation of Bond's arm lifting up as the player's viewpoint zooms in on the watch. You remain vulnerable to enemy gunfire for several precious seconds during the animation, much to the frustration of players.

What most players don't know, however, is that this effect was completely intentional. "I thought it would increase tension and discourage pausing, pushing the player slightly towards playing entire missions in a single sitting," Hollis told me. "I could call it 'lightly sadistic' game design [...] It seems to be a somewhat controversial feature but I like the way it works a lot. It plays with the two realities of 'game time' and 'menu time' in a cute way. It makes more game, because it makes the activity of pausing a part of the decision-making you have to do to play the game successfully. You have to weigh the risks and costs before pressing the Pause button." Strange as it was, the long pause played a big part in immersing the player into the high-risk role of James Bond, since you can't even pause the game until you've fled your enemies to a safe location. "More importantly, when someone is shot dead in this liminal time it is always funny," Hollis told me. "At least, it is funny to me. And, I imagine, to other spectators of the game. Most wonderfully, it is a way to snatch defeat from the jaws of victory near the end of any level."

Hollis told me that he based the delayed watch pause on the same four principles he always uses when making games: Is it fun? Is it funny? Is it self-consistent in the world of the game? and Is it fair?, meaning: "When you die does it feel like it was your fault?" "It doesn't have to seem fair straight away," he told me. "Sometimes I think it is okay if the player has to spend time and come to a realization that the game rule is fair. As one example, the random placement of the scientists in the gas plant push this rule a lot, but it is okay to play with the rules a little bit I think, and to worry the player on the hardest difficulty. The pause menu delay is highly unconventional, and is definitely pushing the issue of fairness. But once you know the rule, it does always feel like your fault when you die in that moment. You can imagine the game speaking to you softly, saying, 'You should not have paused then.'"

In many ways, the watch pause effect encapsulates all that is unique about Hollis's approach to designing games. "Now I think about it more, this feature is very me," he told me. "It ignores convention. And it does tweak the player—albeit in a light and playful way. Nevertheless it is not destructive or wanton. I hope and I trust that all players of *GoldenEye* can ultimately reach an attitude of acceptance here. And if not—guilty as charged. I would do it the same way again."

•

"May I take your photograph?" Jones asked, holding up his camera and flashing his most charming smile at Sally, one of Rare's cleaning staff.

"Sorry, love?" Sally asked in her quaint Midlands accent. Sally was an office favorite, famous for periodically sticking her head into people's cubicles to ask "Any cups?" during her daily missions to collect the mugs and plates that piled up on game developers' desks.

"I'm gathering photographs of people's faces for the game I'm working on," Jones explained. "I've already taken shots of everyone on my team, the IT staff, and the kitchen staff, but I still need more." Although Sally couldn't fathom why anyone would need her face for a video game, considering the only game characters she'd glimpsed on the computer screens at Rare were muscley wolverines and blade-wielding cyborgs, she acquiesced, much to Jones's delight.

While Edmonds and Hollis were building *GoldenEye*'s engine and Hilton and Botwood worked on the levels, Jones had taken the lead on character design. *GoldenEye* was one of the first games to feature actors from a film as recognizable in-game characters. Jones took a precise approach, even going so far as to model multiple versions of Brosnan's face for different levels in the game, with slicked-back hair for his dinner jacket body and more natural hair for other outfits. *GoldenEye*'s final credits list Jones as "Costume Designer," a spot-on designation. His sketches from the era look exactly like the ones you might see in a costuming department, with painstaking details of the locations of zippers and buckles and careful sketches of the hammer and sickle insignia on the Soviet guards' jackets.

Mapping actors' faces onto character models could be difficult, Jones explained to me. "We tried to use the publicity shots of the actors to generate the face maps of the heads," he told me, "but we needed very specific shots for that to make the job easier—you need a full face shot from the front, very flat on, and then you need a side shot, and then we blend them together into one horrific-looking mask" that may not look like the actor at all—plus, the lighting in the publicity headshots the studio provided to Jones, he told me, was all wrong for game textures.

After Jones managed to get the main actors' faces onto the models, he looked to people at Rare to provide faces for the guards. Jones walked around Rare's campus with his massive digital camera taking photos of every willing staffer, starting with the *GoldenEye* team. The face-capturing endeavor, he assured me, was more about getting good face references than about including fun cameos of Rare employees. He would take front, side, and back head shots and stitch them together in a pre-Photoshop pixel painter. As he imported photos of the team members, he sometimes altered them to make them look more like Bond baddies. "I made ghoulish versions of all our faces," Jones told me. "The one of me has big dark circles around the eyes," and Hilton has a gnarly scar.

If you've played the game, you know the most hideous guard face well—bowl haircut, snarly teeth sticking out of his nightmarish face, and thick black eyeliner around his eyes. "Is this creation a foul joke?" an anonymous gamer asked Rare in the late 90s. "Or a foul team member?" Rare's answer noted that this monstrosity "was one of the earliest faces in the game, and stayed in because we never removed it. It is a team member's face, (un)subtly altered, and that particular person also has a less hideous version in the game. He was considered far too attractive to be exposed to the world uncensored." Jones told me he based this hideous guard's face on Botwood's but modified it to look more like Duane Dibbly, a homely character on an English comedy show called *Red Dwarf* that was popular at the time.

When Jones ran out of developers' faces, he recruited Rare's kitchen and cleaning staff, gardeners, IT workers, Tim Stamper's twelve-year-old son Joe, and even a plumber who stopped by the Twycross campus one day. Their names—Sally, Vivien, Pete, Neil, etc.—live on in the game's code. The Stamper brothers, however, declined to include their faces in the game, "perhaps," one reporter wrote, because they were "wary of giving employees the chance to shoot their bosses at close range."

Following his collector impulse, Jones made dozens of character builds in different fun costumes. Soldier and guard uniforms in *GoldenEye* ranged from naval officers to jungle commandos to Siberian Special Forces, adding to the ambience of each level location. Even with all this variety, however, Jones wasn't allowed in the end to include any female characters besides Xenia Onatopp and Natalya Simonova, two of the main characters from the film. "Although I did make Moonraker guards for that Moonraker level at the end, all the female ones were taken out because we couldn't shoot them," Jones later said, due to Nintendo's unease with enabling violence against women. Eventually, he managed to sneak those female Moonraker guards and female civilians (including Sally!) into *GoldenEye*'s multiplayer—the only place you can shoot at women besides the two leads.

Polygons and pixels posed the biggest challenge to Jones's character design process. "All of those textures—all those characters—are literally 42 pixels high by 24 pixels wide," Jones told me, and faces could only use 40 triangles total. "We didn't have Photoshop at this point, so everything you see has been made in Maya in 3D, then you render it and then you put it in Ningen, a texture placement tool, which gave us three options: top left, top right, bottom left. That was all you had to literally stick a texture onto the face." Jones told me if you look at the side of some characters like Natalya, you can see where the textures stretch since he couldn't include side textures on most characters. Polygons were in such short supply that the characters couldn't even have hands or fingers—Jones had to give them block fists, which look really funny when Natalya tries to type on a keyboard. "The lower down the pecking order the character is, the more square his head," Jones told me. "So when you get to Valentin [a side character in the game and film], his head is pretty much a square."

The polygon budgeting process got so ridiculous, Jones told me, that they "had to figure out how many polygons would make breasts as efficiently as possible. It came out to about ten."

"Is that why they're so pointy?" I asked him.

"Let me put it this way," he told me, "That was the best shape we could get because the point would be up here [he gestured on his chest] and it would go out like that, make a little semi-circle and then go in again to another point. That was the kind of research I was doing."

•

Duncan Botwood was battered, bruised, and standing in a smelly neoprene suit attached to the wall by a tangly set of cables. It had been a long day already, and now Jones was asking him to close his eyes.

"You keep flinching when you see where I'm going to hit you," Jones explained. "We'll record a better reaction if you can't see the blow coming."

"Are you sure?" he asked. "Isn't there any other way?"

But Jones was determined, and Botwood was brave. He squeezed his eyes shut and waited for Jones's punch.

While all the *GoldenEye* team members sacrificed large chunks of time for the game, only Botwood sacrificed his body—Botwood had to die a thousand times for *GoldenEye*.

One of *GoldenEye*'s most distinguishing features was its character animations, which were revolutionary for the time in bringing the AI to life and making players feel like they were surrounded by real intelligent enemies. *GoldenEye*'s bad guys roll, run, kneel, and jump while attacking you. They take cover behind boxes and hurl grenades your way, and, most importantly, they react when you shoot them, clutching a nicked shoulder, wincing over a wounded hand, doubling over a groin shot, or dropping to the ground after a bullet to the head. *GoldenEye* was the first game to include location-based hit animations, and every single one of them was recorded by the team's motion capture actor, Duncan Botwood.

Early on, Hollis had envisioned that, unlike *Virtua Cop*, *GoldenEye* would have a large number of pre-recorded moves for each character, including running, staggering, ducking, falling, jumping, and diving. To achieve this ambitious goal, the team had to build an innovative new motion capture system—and find a motion-capture actor to perform all the possible moves. Everyone on the small development team, Botwood said later, "had to wear many hats. One of the hats I got to wear was motion-capture actor."

"I wasn't a specialist," Botwood told me. "I didn't have a degree, so I wasn't buttonholed into a job," plus he had some acting experience from school. "I was more flexible," he explained, "and I would try anything once if it didn't involve personal physical danger—or at least didn't on the face of it involve personal physical danger. If it involved personal physical danger after I started, it was probably too late by then."

And so Botwood ended up doing the game's motion-capture acting, which meant stepping into a "sweaty little room" and putting on a neoprene fitness suit that had never been washed after Rare staff recorded the motion capture for *Killer Instinct*. The suit was hooked up by cables to a capturing unit halfway up the wall, which would sometimes come flying down and hit Botwood if he wasn't careful. "I would do a forward roll, almost fatally entangle myself in the cables, and then I'd have to roll backwards to get the thing from around my neck," Botwood told me. He has said that although the amateur nature of their approach probably shows, it "all came from the heart." Botwood, who had never done any motion-capture acting in his life, truly gave it his all, even adding in the perfect detail of scientists' knees shaking when you point a gun at them and they hold up their hands.

"We went all out for motion capture," Hollis said later. "We probably had two hundred moves, maybe, in *GoldenEye* that could be blended and sliced," organized in a massive list Jones kept with a set of notes he used to describe each move to Botwood as they captured it. Although the guards don't actually say anything in the game, since *GoldenEye* has no voice acting and no onscreen written guard dialogue either, these notes established what their body language was meant to communicate, and gave Botwood a sense of the differing levels of intention and speed with which to act and react. For instance, the notes for "detecting sound" read, "What was that? Did you hear that? What was that sound? Huh? Wassat?" and the notes for "being injured" read, "I'm wounded! I'm hit! Flesh wound. Help!"

Of course, not all the motion-capture moves succeeded in the end, and some proved too complicated to fit onto the cartridge data. "We tried on several occasions to get a good crawl motion-captured, but none were good enough," Botwood wrote on the forums of the old Rare website. "In addition to which, the speed of a crawl is not fast, so having a good crawl that moves at a decent speed is something of a holy grail. We could have had what looked like Deathmatch Luges, but our goal was not to produce something farcical…"

Other animations, like guards scratching their chins or combing back their hair, wouldn't work because the guards had clenched fists and couldn't use their fingers. The team also wanted to let you shoot a gun out of a guard's hands, but that was too difficult to get working with the AI. They did manage, however, to let players shoot off guards' hats. "Once we had a hat-wearing guard, someone wanted to shoot it off," an anonymous *GoldenEye* designer later explained. "So, being the obliging people that we are…"

The hardest moves for Botwood to record were, by far, the guard deaths. "Motion capture data was good at picking up very human movements like flinching" or bracing before a hit, Botwood told *Retro Gamer*, "and you could easily tell the difference between me throwing myself on the floor versus me being pushed to the floor. So I had to stand in position with my eyes shut so I didn't flinch, and [Jones] would walk quietly up to me and shove me hard to make me fall over. Multiply that by eight per position because of covering all the angles and you get a full coverage of animations… and bruises."

Botwood recorded reactions for getting shot from eight different directions. "We even had ropes tied around [Botwood's] waist to pull him off his feet," Jones said in 2018. "We had plenty of soft mats around but I don't think we could have got away with it in today's health and safety-conscious environment."

"Brett took great joy in punching the crap out of me," Botwood told me. But he has no regrets: "All the effort we put in was worthwhile because it led you to believe as a player that there was more going on with the AI than there actually was. If there's one thing we like, it's smoke and mirrors, because it's less work for us."

•

After Jones and Botwood recorded all the motion capture data, Edmonds had to figure out a way to project the data onto the 3D character models. "Because I had no idea what I was doing [and] I was just trying to get this going, I came up with this crazy system to map the joints in the skeleton using a binary system," Edmonds told me, laughing. He had a list of binary identifiers for each joint, which Jones somehow had to remember. "Eventually that became a more user-friendly version," Edmonds told me, in which the left elbow, for instance, was labeled "left elbow" instead of "101."

Jones and Smith then had to pore over all this data as part of their extensive animation clean-up work. The space in which they recorded the motion capture acting had a lot of dead spots, Jones told me, "and the motion would become confused during the capture […] As the movement was captured, the markers would swap names and you would see on the motion capture figure that the hand and hip would swap markers and your stick figure would suddenly have a hip bone wandering off. Other crazy things were [that] the leg would randomly rotate 360 degrees over a couple of frames during a walk. This had to be hand animated again once we got the footage back into [the animation design program]" At that point, because the system picked up way more data than they needed, Jones had to throw out everything but the most essential movement, fix jitters and random jerks, check for firm placement of feet on the ground, and then reduce the amount of detail in the animation curves to cut down on the amount of cartridge space the data would need.

"Unlike animation today," Jones pointed out, "there was no animation rig," a way of isolating a character model's skeleton and displaying it side by side with its fully skinned version. He often had to keep multiple windows open on his screen so he could animate the skeleton and then see the body move in another window. "Of course, we were making this up as we went along, so things that are obvious now we didn't have then," Jones said.

As difficult as the work was, the team kept their senses of humor. Jones showed me a particularly hilarious sheet of notes from the programmers on "how to clean up motion capture," which offers this kind of advice: "If you get lots of straight, coloured lines, then this is good. If you get lots of broken multi-coloured lines then [you're] not going out to play tonight!" The process to smooth out the motion capture animation invites artists to apply "SMOOTH BUTTERWORTH FREQUENCY."

Some cutscenes had to be animated by hand, with no motion capture data at all, like Bond's bungee jump off the top of the dam at the end of the first mission. The extended Bond-Natalya makeout scene that plays during the game's final credits was also hand-animated by Jones, who really went for it. "I had great fun with [that]," Jones told me. "When Natalya lifts her leg at the end—that was [my idea]."

None of the game's animations would have been possible without a key technical innovation by programming whiz Mark Edmonds, who taught himself how to use quaternions—a mathematical way of representing angles and rotations—to transition between different animations smoothly. Modern-day game engines all have quaternions built-in, but when Edmonds first started working on joint blending and animation in 1995, quaternion code libraries didn't exist. "I didn't really know anything about them when I started," he told me. It took him weeks to read library books about them and program a version that worked. When he finally did, the system allowed for smooth transitions between, for instance, an animation of a guard walking into an animation of a guard standing and shooting.

For Edmonds, communicating this innovation is a key detail of the story, he told me, "because it's a mathematical thing, and I'm a mathematician, but also that it was a step above any previous games. I doubt any previous game had ever used quaternions for their animation blending."

"I like seeing things from first principles and coming up with new systems and things that haven't been done before," he told me. "I think some of the stuff people do in games are often at the cutting edge of what people thought of or what people are trying to do. Just always trying to push the boundaries and do new things." And quaternions were just the beginning.

LICENSE TO KILL

AT THE END OF THE 1903 FILM *The Great Train Robbery*—a precursor to the modern Western—the bad guy points and shoots his revolver right at the camera, directly at the audience. Apparently, this shot had such a huge impact on viewers that first they screamed in terror and then they laughed with relief. *GoldenEye* the game—and the James Bond movies on which it's based—opens the same way.

In a sense, "FPS" games long preceded video games. If we're thinking broadly, the earliest "first-person shooters" took the form of coin-operated games in dime museums, carnival fairgrounds, penny arcades, saloons, vaudeville, and cheap variety theatres from about 1890 to 1950. Games like Shoot-a-Lite (1936) pitted players against ducks or safari animals and featured loud banging sound effects. These first-person carnival shooting games are the great-great grandparents of the very first FPS video games that debuted in the 70s and 80s.

In *Maze War*, developed by a trio of NASA high school interns from 1972 to 1973, players wandered a maze of corridors searching for opponents to shoot. Although the game and its many spin-offs featured no story or objectives beyond rudimentary virtual "tag," they were revolutionary for their time. Across the world in Japan, Nintendo and Taito made light gun shooting games around this same time. Nintendo incorporated its Beam Gun technology into a laser clay pigeon shooting range in 1973, and released a light gun shooting game called *Wild Gunman* in 1974. Taito's *Western Gun* in 1975, released by Midway in the US as *Gunfight*, was an early Western-themed video game that allowed shooting duels between two players.

Meanwhile, racing and flight simulator games continued to advance technology that simulated first-person perspective in three-dimensional space. *Battlezone*, a 1980 tank simulator arcade game, pioneered 3D gaming with its black and green wireframe vector graphics, which created the illusion of a 3D depth of field. This marked a big step up from *Maze War*, which moved one static screen at a time in four directions. *Battlezone* had a smoother frame rate and allowed players to move in any direction, paving the way for future open 3D levels like the ones in *GoldenEye*. When *Battlezone* was eventually ported to PCs and home consoles, it became the first 3D mass market game for personal computers—the first commercially distributed FPS.

FPS games took another leap forward in 1991 with id Software's *Catacomb 3-D*, an early fantasy-themed ancestor of *Doom*. "[*Catacomb 3-D*] was more powerful than I expected," id Software co-founder John Carmack said later "We'd watch people creeping around a corner, turning with the arrow keys, and then a door would open, and there would be a big troll right there, and people would scream. They would literally fall out of their chair or jump away from the keyboard. It was a reaction that we'd never seen in any other form of video-gaming," identical to the audience's reaction to *The Great Train Robbery*.

id didn't stop there. In 1992, they released their revolutionary game *Wolfenstein 3D*, often considered the grandfather of FPS games as we know them today. And then, in 1993, id Software released *Doom*, one of *GoldenEye*'s biggest influences. *Doom* pits players against demon monsters invading a space colony; it features fast-paced fighting and introduced co-op and deathmatch multiplayer modes. The instruction manual for *Doom* never refers to it as a "shooter"; instead, it calls itself "a lightning-fast virtual reality adventure" and "an action-oriented slugathon." And indeed, the action in *Doom* felt blisteringly fast—the game cemented FPS conventions like fast run-and-gun gameplay. *Doom* changed the gaming industry overnight, and marked a turning point in the history of video games—it essentially "did for PC games what Elvis or the Beatles did for rock 'n' roll," author Jonathan Hennessey writes in *The Comic Book Story of Video Games*.

GoldenEye borrowed not just general gameplay ideas from *Doom* but also its multiple weapon types, body armor, specific ammo for specific guns, and exploding barrels. It showed players stats after each mission, including kills, items, and completion time. The simple names of *Doom*'s levels, like "Hangar" and "Toxin Refinery," recall *GoldenEye*'s one-word level names like "Depot" and "Facility," but unlike *GoldenEye*, *Doom* had little to offer in the way of narrative. Carmack didn't care much about FPS narrative—he even once said that story in a first-person shooter is about as relevant as story in porn.

Like *Wolfenstein* before it, *Doom* wasn't technically "3D" but rather "2.5D." The game used a clever coding workaround to simulate the illusion of depth and 3D environments by using ray casting and hand-drawn 2D sprites whose scale could change as they traversed the Z axis. True 3D, with polygon-based 3D graphics and a linear perspective, came about later with the SNES's Super FX chip, the N64's Reality Coprocessor, and the PC's *Quake* engine.

To better understand how *GoldenEye* fits into the broader history of FPS games, I consulted John Romero, id Software co-founder and co-creator of the 90s hits *Wolfenstein 3D*, *Doom*, and *Quake*. Romero remembers *GoldenEye* as "the game that brought shooters to consoles finally." Although the FPS was very much a PC-only genre in the mid-90s, *GoldenEye* "had a lot of things in it that games didn't have on the PC," Romero pointed out, like the ability to move the gun around on the screen rather than having to turn your whole body to aim. "There was so much good stuff about that game that nobody still did on the PC for years after that—even *Half-Life* didn't do all the stuff that *GoldenEye* did," Romero told me.

Romero also praised the way the game expanded on the movie's story but kept each mission a manageable, bite-sized segment so as not to overwhelm the player. "You're doing more in the game than you did in the movie," Romero said. "You feel like you're going places, which is what you should feel like when you're 007—you're going all over the world to solve these problems." Nintendo leaned heavily on this "you are Bond" angle in their advertising. The Nintendo website from the era pitches the game like this: "Using the full power of the Nintendo 64, *GoldenEye 007* puts you right into 007's tux and bow tie in a first-person action spectacular."

To fully immerse themselves in the film, the team spent many of their half-hour lunch breaks watching *GoldenEye* in short bursts, looking for inspiration—they watched it about five times in total. It helped that all of them liked Bond films—they'd grown up watching them on the BBC and understood their particular British sense of humor.

The *GoldenEye* team tried to emphasize this "you are Bond" feeling by adding in a camera-spin effect at the beginning of each level and multiplayer match. As the camera spins around Bond's head and then merges the player's point of view with his, the player gets reminded that they are now Bond. The pause screen animation in which Bond lifts his watch up to his face—though frustrating when you're trying to pause while getting shot—also immersed players more fully into the first-person point of view. From the beginning, Hollis wanted to minimize the game's HUD [heads-up display] and visual feedback to further immerse players, and Smith brought this vision to life. "The watch was such an iconic Bond thing that it was a good way to do it," Hilton told me.

Other little touches also add to the feel of being Bond; for instance, you can't run in *GoldenEye*. You always stay cool under pressure. Doak recently tweeted about how one of the first things that struck him after he joined Rare and first saw *GoldenEye 007* was how awesome it feels to rotate and point the gun hand, visually pulling the player into Bond's world. The classic aim style, where the camera stays put as the crosshair moves precisely around the screen, "exudes an aura of measured calm and control," Doak wrote. "It is *very* James Bond. Watching it just feels like Bond is barely moving his head and is gracefully and accurately shooting with minimal effort." If FPS games are generally about immersing the player into the protagonist's point of view, then *GoldenEye* added the additional layer of immersing them into the viewpoint of a calm, cool professional.

•

GoldenEye's Bunker 2 level (the level appears twice) is deliciously challenging, and demands stealthy gameplay to conquer it. The player starts out trapped in a jail cell with ominous stains and bullet holes on the wall. After figuring how to use your watch magnet to grab the cell key off the wall, you'll next need to learn how to navigate the halls of the Russian base by silently karate chopping guards and covertly popping off single shots from your rifle—this level is nearly impossible to beat by running around guns blazing. True stealth masters will take out guards through tiny glass peepholes in doors and eliminate dangerous security cameras with a single shot to the lens. Intricate visual effects like the splintering of glass and the clattering cartridges from your carefully sighted sniper shots heighten the stealth experience.

The degree of realism necessitated by a first-person point of view has for decades driven technical innovation in gaming graphics and hardware. *GoldenEye*'s 3D polygonal graphics represented a cutting-edge leap forward from *Doom* and *Wolfenstein 3D*'s sprite graphics. *GoldenEye*'s graphics felt atmospheric rather than cartoony, and little details like smoke, steam, and shattering glass added to the feeling of realism in each level.

The man who made that smoke and steam—along with the game's weapons, heads-up display user interface, countless textures, as well as several levels, is Ady Smith, an integral lead environmental artist and visual effects artist and the last artist to join the *GoldenEye* team. Aside from Hollis, Smith was the only other team member with previous experience in game design—he moved onto the *GoldenEye* team from *Donkey Kong Country 2*, where he'd worked on Winky the frog as well as backgrounds for the industrial and mine-cart levels.

Smith grew up with a keen passion for drawing; his father was in the Royal Air Force and would bring him home computer paper and pens to scribble with at home. Smith told me he didn't have a great experience in school as a child because it didn't cater to more creative, artistic types like him. He flourished in college, though, focusing on product packaging design and 3D design. After college, he attended Bournemouth's computer visualization and animation master's program (two years before Hilton and Jones), where he survived what he called a "baptism of fire" learning to work with a keyboard and a mouse instead of marker and paper. After he finished his master's, Smith was approached by five different game companies offering him a job as a computer graphic artist; he started at Rare in 1992.

While serving on the *GoldenEye* team, Smith built the level environments for the Jungle and Cradle missions; countless textures for doors, forestry, the tank, and helicopters; almost all the game's weapons; the game's opening animation; and the graphics for the damage and body armor HUD—a feature basically "unheard of at the time." "I wish I'd trademarked the HUD," Smith told me, "because every other console game based off an FPS shooter has incorporated the watch or the graphic health and armor bar."

Smith also handled the game's environmental effects, such as tracer fire, explosions, muzzle flashes, glass shatters, bullet holes, and animated blood. Rather than seeing visual effects as throwaway details, Hollis prioritized them from the start, devoting more space in his game-design document for visual effects than for controls (granted, the N64 controller didn't yet exist in any form at that point). Hollis notes that his list of intended visual effects was "really quite ambitious for what was supposed to be a short project."

The level of detail in *GoldenEye*'s visual effects makes the game feel more interactive and realistic. The explosions, shadows, and even moving clouds in the sky all feel meticulous, creating depth of atmosphere by allowing more player interaction. You can shoot hats off enemies and leave blood stains on their corpses. You can shoot out lights, shatter windows, and write your name on the wall with bullet holes. Smith created muzzle flashes inspired by rewatching and rewinding clips from films like *Heat* and *Aliens*, and the game also features tracer fire, which Smith added to give players an indicator of enemy locations. The detail proved so crucial to making the game fun, Smith told me, that many first-person shooters following *GoldenEye* included tracer fire, too. "They look great and give the player more than a hint but less than complete information about where incoming fire originates from," Hollis told me.

With all these visual details, *GoldenEye* pioneered the sheer destruction players could inflict on the game environment. "The most disappointing thing in first-person shooting games is the fact that, when you fire off vast amounts of ammunition, nothing around you gets damaged at all," a team member wrote on the Rare website at the time, explaining their design choices. "So, we always wanted to make sure that we went that extra step further and allowed the player to do that damage." Players wanted to wreak havoc on everything around them, chairs and tables included.

And so everything explodes in *GoldenEye*, regardless of whether it "should" explode in real life. Computers, tables, chairs, and even small model helicopters all blow up—each with the same size explosion, which, Edmonds pointed out later, "save[d] us having to come up with different destruction effects for every single object."

The developers knew these explosions weren't exactly realistic, but they also knew they added a ton of fun. "Everything explodes in films," Botwood pointed out later. "We were just trying to recreate that atmosphere!"

Hollis knew that, paradoxically, unrealistic elements like the exploding chairs would further immerse players into the game. In his game design document, Hollis defined "realism" as interactivity, not literal realism. "Unthinkingly striving for visual realism is dangerous," he said in 2007. "If all you can think of is reality then you are imprisoned and your hands are tied."

For example, in *GoldenEye* the guards can't spot players through windows, while the player can see and shoot through them. While this may seem like a bug, Hollis says, or at least "unrealistic," it makes for more interesting gameplay since the player gets to feel more like Bond sneaking up on enemies. "Realism isn't relevant to good gameplay," Hollis said in a talk at the 2004 European Developer's Forum. "Only verisimilitude matters. The art is in knowing what you can get away with."

Another choice that prioritized immersion over "realism" had to do with the Rumble Pak. Early in development, the team considered having players reload their weapon by unplugging and reinserting the Rumble Pak on the controller. "Everyone's always wanting there to be some reason for some arbitrary piece of hardware," Doak explained later. "So it was like, 'Can you use this in *GoldenEye*?' Someone said, 'Well, what if you slam in the thing to reload,' because it could detect when it was plugged in. But when we trialed the reload, it was rubbish, so we didn't do it, and it actually became a big joke." Although reloading the in-game gun via a physical action in the real world might have felt more technically realistic, it would have taken the player out of the game (and destroyed lots of controllers to boot).

The team also often sacrificed gritty realism in favor of silliness and humor with elements like the Moonraker outfits, guards with Stormtrooper-level bad aiming, and even the way explosions act on guards. "Because of the way the physics [were] calculated, the forces were transmitted to people nearby quite slowly," Hollis explained in 2013. "So something would explode and then everybody would kind of stand there for a half or quarter of a second, and *then* they'd fly off into the air. And this was hilarious. And we could have fixed it, but instead, wisely, we left it as it was, because it was better being funny."

GoldenEye's sense of humor receives little of the critical attention it deserves. In a lot of ways, the game is a loveable mess, full of weird little quirks and obscure, blink-and-you'll-miss-them gags that make it feel like a hand-crafted work of art rather than a slick, soulless product. "You know that they just went all-out when they made it," John Romero told me. "They loved that game—you can tell. They put their all into all parts of that game. It's why it's great."

GoldenEye's very first little joke comes right at the start of the game, in the form of the opening credits: a black screen covered in white lettering certifying the game, like a copyright. The certification is parodying the British Board of Film Classification, which appears at the beginning of all British films. Instead of "British Board of Film Classification," this one reads "Twycross Board of Game Certification," after Twycross, England, the site of *GoldenEye*'s developer, Rare. And instead of "Suitable only for persons of 12 years and over," as in the film version, this one says "Suitable only for 1-4 persons." Under "vice president" is Martin Hollis's signature, and under "president" is James Bond's, which Hollis did with his left hand. It's a cute little touch, a more interesting way to offer a little copyright info, and an in-joke that only British audiences would get. From the very opening frame, *GoldenEye*'s developers were having fun.

Hollis has noted that the most important question in his first set of pre-development notes was: "What's the appropriate level of Humour?" At one talk, he called humor "a big key to the success of Bond. It really does help relieve the tension of what otherwise could be a very frustrating, intense game."

The game's memorable quirks add a ton of character in a game that's more focused on playful fun than on seeming grim, slick, or cool. The name of the game's no-guns multiplayer mode—"Slappers Only"— isn't slick or cool, and neither is the "big head" toggleable gameplay setting, which gives all the characters enormous heads. Playing in these modes doesn't feel like murder at all, but rather like pure silliness. "In our head, Bond wasn't a ruthless killer—he was a slightly silly British agent," Hilton told me, like the Roger Moore version of Bond that most of the team had grown up watching. "He doesn't take himself too seriously and we don't take him too seriously."

Doak pointed out that *GoldenEye* also riffs on Bond's double entendre puns, which allowed Doak to work what he calls "puerile humor" into Moneypenny's flirtatious pre-mission briefings, like, in the Caverns level: "Doing a spot of spelunking? Well, don't mess your trousers up, James," or, in the Statue level: "Be careful with that chopper, James," which makes way more sense if you know that "chopper" is British slang for penis. Moneypenny's briefings weren't the only place for naughty humor; although some have speculated that the "DD" in the DD44 Dostovei pistol's name came from "David Doak," Doak himself assured me that it's actually a joking reference to double-D-sized bras.

On another late evening of playtesting, Hilton slunk stealthily down the corridor of Bunker and loaded up the throwing knife to take out a hapless guard patrolling the base. He aimed, drew back the weapon, and threw it— only to see a fence from the Depot level go flying down the hall and knock over the guard. A bug in the code had swapped the fence model in for the knife model. "Should we keep that as a weapon?" they jokingly asked each other, then held a fence-throwing deathmatch together because it was just so funny.

The team made a surprising number of weapon decisions this way—simply for humor's sake. For this reason, *GoldenEye*'s weapons often feel more like characters than props—and Hollis and the team thought of them that way. Each of *GoldenEye*'s diverse weapons has a unique feel created by its sound effect, rate of fire, damage inflicted, rate of reload, and appearance on screen.

The team originally modeled the game's weapons on real guns and accurate weapon behaviors. None of the team members had any personal experience with guns, so they had to rely on a "well-thumbed" large-format picture book called *Firearms of the World*, Doak told me. And, of course, they had John Woo films and *Heat* to fall back on for further inspiration. Smith modeled all the weapons except the shotgun, rocket launcher, and Soviet rifle, which Hilton built. Since the artists had such limited polygons to use for the guns, they had to keep them very low-res, with a maximum of 64-bit textures. And the artistic reference for the hand holding the guns? It's Botwood's.

The reloading action around clips—revolutionary for its time—and onscreen gun sway provided a nice touch of realism. An online resource called the *GoldenEye* Arms Reference explains that in *GoldenEye*, "[t]he player is not a perfectly frigid robot, and when standing still his weapon and the scene in front of him will slowly rock with his breathing, pulse, and the tension of his muscles. This becomes particularly obvious when using a powerful sight, especially that of the sniper rifle."

Other weapon behaviors are less tied to realism. For instance, using two guns at once—aka dual wielding or guns akimbo—is reckless and impractical in real life but feels incredibly badass in the game. *GoldenEye*'s particular flavor of dual-wielding badassery was another John Woo inspiration. In 1995, as Hollywood reporters hemmed and hawed over Bond's continued relevance or lack thereof, Woo himself actually once offhandedly suggested letting Bond dual-wield in *GoldenEye* the film. The game's inclusion of dual-wielding was nothing new, of course—dual-wielding emerged in games as early as Nintendo's *Sheriff* in 1979, and many games before and since *GoldenEye* have featured the stunt. But as common as it might be in popular culture, the last time it served as a practical fighting strategy dates back to the 18th century, when guns took so long to reload that pirates like Blackbeard might carry up to six loaded pistols at once.

In his original game design document, Hollis planned for *GoldenEye* to include Bond's sidearm of choice, the Walther PPK (with a silencer), along with a number of other weapons of varying sizes and types. In the end, Smith told me, the team decided which guns to include based on what they saw in the film and what looked fun and cool in their picture book. For melee mode, they opted for a karate chop (or slap, depending on how you look at it) instead of a punch because straightening Bond's fingers out proved easier for the artists than folding them into a fist.

The game's final collection of weapons included powerful revolvers like the Cougar Magnum, punishing submachine guns like the RCP-90, a particle beam laser, and even James Bond's trusty Walther PPK (renamed the PP7 in the game due to trademark issues). The game also crammed in a vast array of explosive weapons, including grenades; a rocket launcher; and timed, proximity, and remote mines. One of the most common guns in the game, carried by most guards, was the KF7 Soviet assault rifle, a reliable weapon based off the Kalashnikov AK-47, the gun you see all the bad guys holding in *GoldenEye* the movie. The gun is one of the most evenly balanced in the game, offering a rapid-fire burst for crowd control as well as a scope with a decent zoom for sniping.

The team's model for weapon balance was *Doom*, which they often played during their lunch breaks, Smith told me. The main way they achieved balance in the game's arsenal was by assigning every gun a different rate of fire, accuracy metric, damage level, and magazine size. The shotgun, for instance, which the team included simply because *Doom* had one, was devastating at close range but weaker at a distance, and had molasses-slow firing and reload rates. "We tried to make sure that you didn't necessarily get a single bullet going in the center of the reticle when you do a shotgun blast," Botwood said, "because if you know you can snipe with it, it breaks the whole immersion of it. You can snipe with the pistol, but it doesn't zoom in to help you."

GoldenEye's actual sniping weapon, of course, was its revolutionary sniper rifle. *GoldenEye* wasn't technically the first game to feature a sniper rifle—the third-person Mac OS shooter *MDK* beat them to that by just a few months, but this was a case of parallel invention rather than inspiration. Smith constantly urged Hollis and Edmonds to include one, nagging them about it every few months until finally Edmonds added it in. "Because of those two people," Hollis emphasized, "there's an incredible feature in that game which is kind of the set piece—it's a highly visual moment for the game that a lot of people remember. And a lot of people who aren't so confrontational really like the sniper's rifle."

Indeed, taking out guards from hundreds of feet away feels deeply satisfying and spy-like; the sniper rifle perfectly emphasizes the game's stealth play style. The weapon took two weeks to program, Hollis said.

"The actual view distance itself wasn't a particular problem," Edmonds told me, "but [we] did have to implement some relative coordinate origin shifting to prevent wobble."

If the sniper rifle was the game's most elegant weapon, the Klobb was easily its least. The Klobb, a machine pistol, is a wonderfully, notoriously, legendarily awful gun, and a fan favorite for that reason. The Klobb is loud and conspicuous and somehow feels lightweight, like a toy. It offers a little over half as much damage as a slap, and that's assuming you can make contact with this wildly inaccurate gun. The Klobb made its way into the game because the developers wanted the guns to all look, feel, and sound very different from each other. "For the guns to be different, they needed a kind of character, and the Klobb had a character of just [having] a small magazine," Botwood told me. "It's a chattery, jumpy gun and it comes into its own in one-hit kill death matches because it can [spray] the entire corridor very quickly."

The team members also just thought it was funny, Hilton told me, adding that at one point, the game included an even worse version of the Klobb—a version so bad you couldn't hit anything at all. "It was hilarious, but in the end we thought, 'We can't do this to people,'" Hilton told me.

Smith modeled the Klobb after the Škorpion vz. 61, a real-life, cheaply made Soviet machine pistol. But after Nintendo's lawyers, out of fear of lawsuits from gun manufacturers, decided toward the end of the development process that the team couldn't use any actual weapon names in the game, the Klobb became the Spyder. After Nintendo had already printed 800,000 instruction manuals with the name "Spyder," Nintendo's legal department called Rare and told them they had to change the name again, since "Spyder" was already the name of a type of paintball gun.

The legal department emphasized that the gun's new name needed to pass a worldwide trademark search, but Rare didn't have time to conduct one, so they had to pick a name unique enough to guarantee it didn't belong to anything else already. Thus, the gun was re-christened the "Klobb," after Ken Lobb, a Nintendo of America employee who worked with the team for the last nine months of development. Lobb "was a big champion of Rare," Botwood noted years later. "He was a whirlwind of a man—so enthusiastic, loves games, totally apparent, and we did him a huge disservice by labeling the loudest, most inaccurate gun after him."

Hollis has expressed similar playful regret, telling an *Edge* reporter in 2014 that "I do slightly regret naming such a poor weapon after [Lobb], since I am tremendously fond of the man. He is astonishingly enthusiastic about games, even after years of working in the industry. It's a little unfair that we named such a useless weapon after him. And for that I am sorry."

Lobb doesn't take any of this personally at all, however—in fact, just the opposite. "I'm thrilled that there's a gun in *GoldenEye* named after me; it's an honor of a lifetime," he said later. "In one-hit kills, it's the best gun in the game. It's also the first gun you could dual wield."

The game's most controversial weapons weren't any of the powerful guns or the massive grenade launcher but rather the knives. The game's throwing knives inflicted a huge amount of damage in total silence and could be picked up and used again. "We have throwing knives in the game because they're hilarious," Doak told me, even though they aren't very Bondian per se. "They were very nearly cut at the last moment because there was a tragic murder in Japan" involving a hunting knife, Doak added. The team received a fax from Nintendo asking them to take out the knives, arguing that a knife felt more offensive than a gun because it meant "too much murder in the close distance"—an explanation that tickled the team. "We just loved that phrase," Doak told me, laughing. "It became a phrase we would use. Murder in the far distance is great—knock yourself out all day long, but not murder in the close distance." In the end, the throwing knives—which could be hurled at an enemy from down the hall—got to stay in the game while the hunting knife was removed.

It wasn't the only weapon cut from the game, either. Leftover in the game's code remain several other unused weapons and weapon parts, like a dart gun inspired by *Moonraker* and an exploding fire extinguisher. A sneak preview in *Nintendo Power* #93 had teased the taser, which ended up getting cut from the campaign due to time and space constraints but remained available with the all-weapons cheat. In addition, a considerable number of gadgets still exist in the code that never made it into the final game, including, among others, a flare gun, a keyring that emits knockout gas, and an exploding pen.

The team also had to cut out a firing range that Smith had built as a kind of mini-game, with one range for pistols, another for rifles, and one for the sniper and rocket launcher, with timed accuracy tests and target-shooting games that could unlock new weapons. Smith's shooting range looked just like the one from Q branch in the movie, Smith told me—he duplicated the hallways and made the floor transparent so it looked like you had a mirror image of the galleries. But this double geometry would have slowed the frame rate down, and the team needed the cartridge space for multiplayer, so it had to wait until an eventual appearance in *Perfect Dark* (2000). Besides, they had plenty to keep their hands full with finishing up *GoldenEye*, which was starting to prove more complex than any of the team members had originally thought it might be.

THE MEN WITH THE
GOLDEN GUNS

"COME ON, HAVE A GO," Edmonds urged Hollis. Game design usually isn't a linear process—halfway through the development process, it's typical that you don't have a game at all yet, Hollis has said. But halfway through *GoldenEye*'s development, they did have a testable game, and Edmonds invited Hollis to do a very early playtest of the Bunker level.

"I just remember not feeling anything, and I didn't say anything," Hollis said years later, but "I guess my face said everything." "It was absolutely diabolical," he added. "The movement was completely dead, the sound effects were completely dead, the gun was dead on the screen—it had no reaction, no movement. There was no auto-aim—there was a cross-hair that you had to line up perfect. There was no juice at all in the game. And essentially it took circa a year to add layer on layer of little movements, little sounds, little reactive graphical effects on textures when you shoot, little glints on the gun. Layer upon layer upon layer of little effects just to make it feel more punchy and more like the game was actually listening to what you were doing."

It took a lot of long hours to get there: long even by the standards of an industry notorious for overworking its workers. "When I was at Rare," Doak said later, "we used to spend all of our time there—I mean, literally, all of your time there. You would get up in the morning and go to work and on a slow day, you would go home about 9:00 [or after midnight during crunch, he told me]. The average working day was twelve hours, and you usually went in on the weekend too."

Jones recently put it like this: "It was definitely a work work work, work some more, do some work, work a bit more, are you still at work? Yeah. Then do some more work."

"We really wanted to make it a knockout game," Hollis said in 2020. "That meant we had a huge amount to deliver in a short amount of time."

And working long hours can be as addictive as a drug, Doak has noted, especially when you're surrounded by a team of talented people making something exciting, watching it get better every day. "We all kind of suffered from the imposter syndrome, in that we all thought we were really lucky to be having a chance to work on it at all," Doak said in 2018. "We were really worried that it wouldn't be any good, and we'd let everyone down."

The team's imposter syndrome came partly from their youth and inexperience—everyone on the *GoldenEye* team was in their late 20s or early 30s and mostly single, something Rare specifically looked for, since it meant their employees wouldn't have a life outside of work. Rare's workplace culture also strongly encouraged long hours. The company's whole ethos had always been about scrappy workaholic excellence, starting with their earliest days as Ultimate Play the Game. Into the 90s, the Stamper brothers themselves continued to maintain long hours, and around Rare there was little respect for employees who only worked nine to five. "You were promoted if you were dedicated, and by dedicated, I mean, do you stay long hours and work yourself hard?" Botwood told Eurogamer.

The pressure was always on—Rare even fostered a sense of friendly competition between development teams. "A driving principle for the quality of what was done [at Rare] was that although we were making games that were going out to compete internationally, we were actually just competing with the team across the hall," Doak told me. "It was all about doing something better than what the other teams at Rare were doing, and that was a real driver." The teams at Rare were known as the Bond team, the Killer team (for *Killer Instinct*), the Diggers team (for *Blast Corps*), and the Dream Team—the top-notch group who had created *Donkey Kong Country* and were now working on "Project Dream," which eventually became *Banjo-Kazooie*.

As hard as the team worked, they never refer to that work as torturous or miserable. "I was in heaven," Botwood told me of the *GoldenEye* development years. "I was living in a bed and breakfast across the road from work. I would get up at the crack of dawn, like 7:30. I would have my breakfast at the B and B. I would go across the road and I wouldn't come back until midnight. I was working stupid hours because I was so excited to be working in video games."

Likewise, *GoldenEye* composer Grant Kirkhope told me he "loved every second" of his time at Rare. "That golden period of time at Rare was just unbeatable," he told me. "We were on a real mission to be the best in the world. And Tim and Chris Stamper were just fantastic bosses. Those two brothers were completely in tune, never disagreed, and were just brilliant."

Rare's Twycross headquarters consisted of Manor Farmhouse, an elegant but slightly run-down dilapidated 18th-century mansion, as well as several barns, outbuildings, and a crew of roosters and chickens that wandered the property—one got run over in the parking lot at some point, Jones told me. As Rare expanded, they began repurposing the farm's barns into development studios, and each ten- to fifteen-member team had its own barn. Each team member's key gave them access only to their own barn, adding to the feeling of secrecy and friendly competition between teams. Inside the *GoldenEye* barn, *Pulp Fiction* and *Blade Runner* posters hung from the exposed brick walls, and a life-size cardboard cut-out of Pierce Brosnan as James Bond stood in one corner of the barn, a toilet paper roll sheathing his pistol. Hilton's shelves were decked out with model sports cars, and Doak hung up a Teletubbies poster with moveable character magnets that the team would pose in compromising positions.

Aside from the Teletubbies, the barn offered few distractions. "It was a fairly monastic, institutionalized life" at Rare, Doak told me, and the barns were generally quiet and busy most of the time. Work began every day promptly at 9 a.m. and often lasted well past 9 p.m., with a quick lunch break of homemade puddings and custards from the canteen.

"If you wanted a cup of tea or a coffee, you would walk to the canteen across the courtyard, and people would regularly go and bring back a tray of drinks" for everyone else, Jones explained to me.

Doak and Hollis both smoked, but this was prohibited on Rare's premises, so the two would periodically walk to a field across the street from the Rare campus throughout the day for their smoke breaks. Later in development, two visitors from Nintendo's Japanese office—Keisuke Terasaki and Kenji Okubo—began to visit the Rare barn to work on the Japanese translation and localization of the game, and Terasaki smoked, too. "[Smoking] was really frowned upon," Doak remembered later, laughing, "but then Mr. Terasaki came, and he just wanted to smoke a cigarette since that's what he did all the time, so we were allowed to go and take Mr. Terasaki out for cigarette breaks."

Once a week, at around 8:00 pm, a group of about a dozen Rare staffers would gather together at a tiny curry shop called The Sizzling in Ashby, a small town up the road from Twycross, for beers and curry. "[Curry night] was an important social event of the week," Doak told me. He recently tweeted that 1990s game development at Rare "was largely fueled by Poppadoms, Chicken Shashlik and Cobra Lager."

The team used to get takeout together in the evenings and on the weekends, and they bonded over their shared "geeky tastes," Edmonds told me—films, games, and, of course, *Star Trek*, which inspired Easter Eggs like red-shirted civilians in the Streets level, a nod to the fact that the characters in red shirts on *Star Trek* were always the first ones to die.

On late nights working at the barn, they entertained each other with "sleep-deprived" Sean Connery impressions and other goofy antics. A small, sound-proofed recording room beside one of the composer's desks provided the perfect place to go and hide, Doak noted later, "since no one would dare open the door in case you were recording." Sometimes team members would take time-outs in the room just to "stand and shout and swear," he added.

Spending all day and most of the night in the barn brought the team closer together. The people you worked with at Rare were your "best mates," Kirkhope told me. "When you feel like you're part of something special, you want to not let anybody down," he said. "There's a real sense of camaraderie."

Edmonds described the team as "a little family of people making [a] game." Strikingly, almost none of the team members I spoke with remember any arguments at all. Think about that for a moment: When's the last time you worked with seven other people on a three-year project without having a single argument?

"I can only really remember one argument in the Bond team that was heated, and that was about how to do tracer fire," Hollis told me. He started discussing it with Hilton and Edmonds, and ten minutes later the whole team had converged on the room, sharing their many different opinions about the ideal amount of visibility and realism. "This level of conflict was exceptional for the *GoldenEye* project," Hollis told me. "I think this is remarkable given the amount of pressure we were under, the long hours we worked and the fact the project was nearly three years long."

"We were well aware of how lucky we were to be working at Rare, working on a Nintendo 64 game, working with some of the best software in the industry, working with some of the most talented people in the industry, and working with an IP like James Bond," Hilton told me. "None of us took that for granted for one second. I couldn't believe how lucky I was to be in that position."

Again and again, *GoldenEye*'s developers have attributed the game's success to the team dynamic of the development process. Over the years, Hollis in particular has repeatedly rejected auteur theory—the idea that a game reflects the artistic vision of a single individual, like the director of a movie. When it comes to game development, Hollis has said he privileges a democratic approach, a "shared vision rather than solitary vision" that resonated profoundly with his *GoldenEye* team members. During my conversations with each of them, they all praised Hollis's leadership style.

"There wasn't a top-down hierarchy," Jones told me. "It was like a scrum talk where everybody has a valuable opinion."

"The team was fairly flat in terms of organizational structure, and people trusted each other's judgment," Doak told me. Even when he gave a major talk at the 2012 Game Developers Conference, Hollis polled all the team members for their perspectives and wove them throughout his address.

Without Hollis's flat team structure, Smith told me, the game might have ended up feeling like just any other generic first-person shooter. Although Rare had an unspoken hierarchy, with programmers at the top, then game designers, then artists, then musicians, then QA, Hollis didn't follow that, Smith told me. "We were all developers, we were all wanting to make a really good game, and we all had a drive and an input and say on how that game was made. So without one of those people, *GoldenEye* wouldn't be the game that it would have been."

•

Camera bulbs flashed and a quiet excitement settled over the presentation hall as Ken Lobb, dressed in khaki pants and a simple T-shirt, with a lapel mic clipped to his collar, strode across the stage to a Nintendo 64 console positioned at the top of a display podium.

"Let's get on with the demo," he told the excited crowd. "We're going to do something a little different than we've usually done. Instead of showing you a video tape, which we'll do later on, we'd like to give you a feeling of what it's like when people are actually playing, so we're going to do a live demo."

Onto the stage walked two young employees of Nintendo of America's Treehouse product development division, one wearing a backwards baseball cap. The men sat on the stage, legs dangling over the edge, facing the audience. One picked up a controller. Lobb turned on the console and, for the first time ever, the opening sounds of *Super Mario 64* made their way into the ears of the public: "It's a me, Mario!" On a huge screen at the front of the room, the 3D castle courtyard of *Super Mario 64* spread itself before the audience, who began murmuring and oohing and aahing with excitement. They burst out into laughter as one of the testers ran Mario around in a circle, and got so rowdy during a demo of the icy penguin slide race that Lobb had to raise his voice into the mic just to be heard.

The unveiling of *Super Mario 64* at the May 1996 E3 convention in Los Angeles was a big moment. At the time, game makers were dismayed about what had been a slow couple of sales years industry-wide, and they feared the possibility of another total market crash. But with the revolutionary N64, it seemed like Nintendo might yet again save video games, just as it had after the Atari crash of 1983. The company even hired Cirque de Soleil for their party, sending men on stilts ambling through the Biltmore Hotel's packed ballroom while acrobats executed stunts overhead.

It was in this intense setting, at E3 1996, that the American public caught their next glimpse of *GoldenEye*, in a promotional video of all of Nintendo's upcoming games. The video featured a clip of *GoldenEye* set in a very early (and still on-rails) version of the Silo level. In the short video, the player holds an assault rifle and moves slowly along a scripted spline path, shooting at guards along the way. In a level that would eventually become all about moving rapidly, trying to beat the clock before a rocket launch, it's very strange now to see such a different game feel here—one where the player has no control over Bond's movement, only his gun, and the camera sets the (slow) pace entirely. How did the game change so drastically just one year later, when it was released in August 1997?

By spring of 1996, the team had already missed several deadlines, and Hollis understood that Nintendo could cancel the project entirely. "It was clear to everyone Nintendo wasn't interested in something so-so," Hollis told Game Developer (formerly Gamasutra). "Looking back, I imagine there were lots of very serious, ongoing discussions about cancelling the project."

A year and a half into development, the team finally got access to the Nintendo 64's hardware. Initial relief quickly gave way to disappointment, however, when the team discovered that the processor wasn't nearly as powerful as they had hoped—only about three quarters of what Nintendo had told them it would be. Both ROM and RAM size presented issues, and the texture graphics were another big problem. The N64 allowed perspective-correct, filtered textures—an advantage over other consoles and a capability that resulted in more solid-looking game worlds. But the N64's limited cache meant that most of the game's textures had to stay under a measly 32x32 or 64x64 pixels. "One of [Hilton's] bugbears and one of his very tight constraints was the size of the textures he had to make," Hollis said later.

Essentially, if the art got too complicated, the levels would slow down or even crash. And so the team had to balance memory between graphics and performance speed. As Hilton built the levels, he divided textures equally between the level background, the characters, and the props. Then, if the level couldn't run at a decent frame rate, the artists had to find ways to simplify the visuals, essentially by cutting the game's textures in half.

First, they trimmed back colors. Since RGB color textures cost more processing power, much of *GoldenEye* is in black and white. Hilton could achieve double the resolution if he designed levels in grayscale, adding color accents back into polygons by hand, vertex by vertex. "The classic example is the Complex multiplayer level,"

Hilton told me, "which is entirely black and white with a few bits of color thrown in, which is just vertex coloring. I was trying to get very high performance since it was our first multiplayer level that was designed, and I was trying to get every kind of conceivable space into it so we could test it all out."

Botwood still remembers squashing down textures and stripping out colors in Photoshop. "We had to get very technical and very specific about what exactly you wanted out of this texture, and you'd be editing the individual pixels to make sure that it worked correctly," Botwood told me.

Artists could also conserve memory by reusing assets. For instance, the radar disc in multiplayer mode reuses the oil drum texture. Hilton's creativity truly saved the day when it came to texture caches. "I vaguely remember being disappointed seeing the [N64] tech demos running on the first development consoles," Edmonds said in 2018. "But once our own artists got going onto the project, they managed to make the graphics look good!"

In the end, "*GoldenEye* pretty much exhausted the performance of [the N64]," Doak said in 2004. "It was hard to push it further." The game crammed in an incredible amount considering its tiny size. The entire *GoldenEye* cartridge is only 12 MB large, which means that if you have a 64 GB phone, you could fit 5,333 copies of *GoldenEye* on it. In one talk, Hollis pointed out that games today contain individual textures as large as all of *GoldenEye*. The game was originally set to be ten times bigger, so over the course of the development process, the team constantly compressed everything. Jones's old notes reveal how technically and mathematically the artists had to think, with notes like "cutuprgb.nomm. Normally subtract 1 from start size for every cut (no. of end tiles) x (end size) <- (no. of end tiles) x (end size) + 1 - (no. of end tiles)."

Level architecture had to respond to the N64's hardware constraints, too. The Dam and Cradle levels, for instance, were rendering nightmares since they featured large open spaces with long views, which required a significant memory budget to display and overtaxed the N64's hardware, resulting in a sluggish frame rate.

Hilton dreaded designing the Cradle level so much that he and co-designer Ady Smith saved it for last. "That was a total nightmare," he told me, "because it was floating in the middle of the air, open steel framework," but had to look that way to match the movie's climactic final scene. He added fog in levels like these so that the N64 wouldn't have to draw everything at once. Likewise, he had to add doors, bookcases, and corners into Archives to make it look like a bigger building in order to give the N64 enough processing time. "There's lots of spaces where we had to put in a door that closed because once it closed I could turn everything off behind it," Hilton told me. Hollis had created a portal rendering system for *GoldenEye*, which meant that every level was divided up into smaller "rooms" and the console only drew the room the player was currently in, not everything outside of it. Closing one door and cutting off the ability to see it at all before opening another let the game run faster—a technique used, for instance, in the dual-gated truck entrance on Dam.

To this day, the developers still seem haunted by the game's frame rate—they often bring it up guiltily in interviews and even apologize for how slow certain levels ran. The team wanted to get as much performance out of the N64 as possible—ideally 30 frames per second, but at the end of the day, *GoldenEye* performs at an average 15-30 frames per second. It's a slow number, but not for 1997. And if they had to sacrifice frame rate for more detailed level art, then it's a deal Hollis came to terms with. "Frankly," he said in 2004, "I think the benefit from having 50% more triangles in the backgrounds outweighed the cost of running at 20Hz in some places. I think the benefit of being able to have eight characters on screen [in multiplayer] outweighs the cost of running at 10Hz. The benefit of having thick smoke outweighs the cost of running at 10Hz. I don't think the same decisions are correct today, with the more powerful hardware."

•

The tiny office in the *Killer Instinct* barn had filled, standing room only, with artists, programmers, and game designers, all staring at a tiny CRTV. On the screen, Mario leapt and swam and sprinted around Princess Toadstool's castle grounds—all in glorious, gorgeous, full 3D. *Super Mario 64*'s E3 debut had wowed crowds ready to be wowed, but now, back home in Twycross, it was wowing Rare's brilliant game developers, who watched the game with more critical eyes.

"How'd they do that?" an artist would ask, pointing out a certain 3D model or animation. Hollis and another Rare staffer brainstormed aloud about how Miyamoto's team must have programmed the hits for Mario's slide move, and how they got the 3D camera to work.

The day Rare got *Super Mario 64*, Doak told me, the company's staff spent hours forensically unpacking the game bit by bit. "And it being Rare, you just knew that in that room there's the talent to dissect this thing and probably do it better," Doak said.

That's exactly what Hollis and the team wanted to do. "Somewhere in the second third of the project, with my enthusiastic encouragement, the team formed a consensus that the goal was free movement," Hollis told me. Shortly after the 1995 Shoshinkai trade show, the *GoldenEye* team had realized that a rail shooter would soon be obsolete. Players craved the freedom of exploring worlds, and *Super Mario 64* now clearly demonstrated just how fun that could be. The team had also spent many evenings playing networked *Doom*, which had made them wonder even early on if they could make an open 3D version of *GoldenEye*. Botwood, for instance, remembers the team doing a free movement test as early as the summer of 1995, just six months into development.

Although *Virtua Cop* still provided their main model, Hollis and Edmonds just couldn't settle for a game on rails. "We all really enjoyed playing [*Doom*] and [having] the freedom of moving around," Edmonds told me, and Hollis was thinking ambitiously about how to extend their 3D graphics capabilities beyond *Doom*. "In *Doom*, you can't look up and down in the initial version of the game," Edmonds told me, "whereas with a full 3D engine that we had on the Nintendo 64," the team could make that happen in *GoldenEye*. "Being able to move around freely and look up and down was quite an innovation for us at the time," Edmonds added.

Indeed, once the team finally saw what the N64 console could do, they began to realize its full potential. The N64 could render 3D polygonal graphics from any orientation and direction, opening up the possibilities for a totally 3D game, and the revolutionary analog control stick on the N64's controller made precision aiming possible. The team had made the big decision to take *GoldenEye* off rails, effectively creating the game as we know it now. Although an on-rails version would have taken less time and allowed the team to release the game closer to the launch of the N64, they knew they'd made the right decision once they got a prototype working, and they quietly abandoned an earlier proposal to keep the on-rails function as an extra mode.

Even after *GoldenEye* came off the rails, it retained many influences from *Virtua Cop*, as noted in a provocatively titled Retro Collect article called "Is *GoldenEye 64* Actually an Arcade Game?" Features like location-dependent hit damage, the sniper rifle's zoom, reloading your gun, penalties for killing innocents, and even the ability to shoot through glass all retained the feel of *Virtua Cop*. The Silo, Dam, and Train missions still feel a little like a rail shooter, with a fairly linear level design consisting of pockets of areas to clear, with enemies popping in and out of cover. Hollis also attributes to *Virtua Cop* the amount of effort the team put into animation; the amount of action in the gameplay; and the control scheme. The game's final controls retained a lot from the on-rails testing, like the ability to aim anywhere on the screen by pressing "R," which Botwood pointed out to me basically switches the game into "*Virtua Cop* mode." "A lot of the controls came from that initial testing," Edmonds told me. "Because it was going to be a fixed area, we had a lot of aiming the gun anywhere on the screen, and then that stayed once you could move around freely."

Of course, for the first big chunk of development, the team had to design the controls with no controller. "We had no idea what the [Nintendo 64 controller] would be at all" during the early development period, Hollis said in 2012. "There was no certainty, but there was a rumor that there was going to be an analog stick. That was all I knew." The team made do with a "butchered" Sega Saturn controller for playtesting and hoped for the best.

When they did finally gain access to an N64 controller, the team tried every control method they could imagine. In the end, their biggest inspiration came, yet again, from *Super Mario 64*. "There was a lot of talk about the controls, because there was this new analog stick and people weren't used to using it," Edmonds told me. The analog stick represented a massive innovation, offering console FPS players as much precision in aiming as PC gamers had with their mice—maybe even more so, since the stick re-centers while the mouse has to be continually moved back. So, since most new N64 gamers had grown accustomed to the control scheme of *Super Mario 64*, Edmonds and Hollis "were basically trying to create some controls that would match that, that would be familiar to someone who had only played Mario," Edmonds told me. The resulting default control scheme, Edmonds noted, allows you to play one-handed, with the single stick controlling both player movement and gun movement for a simple, tight game feel.

GoldenEye's default control setting meant holding the middle nub of the N64's three-pronged controller in the left hand and using the left thumb to move your character around on screen with the controller's single analogue joystick. The left index finger fired the gun trigger while the right hand, holding the righthand prong of the controller, punched the reload button and switched guns (with the right thumb), and aimed the gun (with the right index finger).

GoldenEye's ability to translate the smoothness of a PC's mouse controls and the fun of a light gun shooter's aiming scheme onto a console marked a true breakthrough. The developers worked tirelessly on a deliberate rhythm for *GoldenEye*'s core aiming and shooting mechanics—they wanted the game to "feel" great, from the animations to the camera sway to the sense of each gun's weight. "We want it to seem realistic," Botwood told *Nintendo Power*. "We want it to be a genuine experience, and that includes having Bond move like a real person."

In the *Nintendo 64 Anthology*, Hollis said that the best moment he experienced working on *GoldenEye* was when Edmonds got the weapons to move accurately. "It took more than a year to get there," Hollis said. "I played it so many times and the movement seemed flat, so when he finally got it right, I was genuinely happy."

Kirkhope told me that the *GoldenEye* team made games that they themselves would want to play, focusing on game feel and gameplay rather than polish. "That's what it's like to be a great gamemaker—to know just what other people want to feel like," he said.

"We spent a lot of time getting the auto-aim just the right amount of help," Hilton told me, "and trying to get the levels to play nicely and getting the movement to feel right."

"The auto aim was pretty crucial," Edmonds told me, since the controller offered no easy way to aim up and down on a vertical axis. The team modeled their auto-aim, then, on *Doom*'s, which auto-aims vertically since you can't move your gun up or down in that game. "So our auto-aim was similar for mainly shooting up & down (as your stick by default would turn sideways & move forwards), and it was a D-Pad or buttons for looking up/down," Edmonds said. "And then the auto aim was handy for different difficulties," since it can be turned down on harder difficulties. "On Agent, it would just shoot anything roughly that you're looking at and then on the 00 Agent it was only doing very vertical aiming so you had to be a bit more precise on your turning," Edmonds noted. He and Hollis also fiddled with the durations of animations and transitions between them to give players the best possible experience with aiming.

Even though the team put a Herculean amount of effort into the game's default control settings, they also built in a whopping eight other control scheme options to accommodate many different play styles. Half of these control schemes allowed you to play with two controllers, one in each hand, which prefigured contemporary dual analog joystick controllers. Botwood himself played exclusively with the dual controller mode once they added that in. "*GoldenEye 007* was one of the first, if not *the* first console game to include options for dual analogue controls," he noted later.

As Doak put it in a Tweet, "we basically invented the dual analog controller."

id Software co-founder and Doom creator John Romero said *GoldenEye*'s controls were one of the first things he noticed about the game when he played it back in 1997. "It was really cool, really fun to play," he told me. "I don't play very many console games, but people had been talking about how good that one was, like how the control felt so good," he said. Romero called *GoldenEye*'s control scheme one of its most important contributions to console first-person shooters. "Control of a first-person shooter is critical," he said, noting the importance of the friction you feel as a player, the speed of the stick when you're aiming, and the responsiveness of the buttons. "If the game feels bad on the controller, I don't care how cool it looks." *GoldenEye*'s controls, Romero said, felt natural, and it's still a game that designers reference for control, decades later: "People have always referenced that if you're going to put a shooter on console, then you need to make sure to play *GoldenEye* and understand how that works, because they did it perfectly."

ANTI-GAME DESIGN

"WHY IS THIS TAKING SO LONG?" Hollis asked Botwood. For two weeks, he'd been working to set up AI navigation markers across *GoldenEye*'s levels—a painstaking and laborious hand-coding process.

"Martin, you asked me to connect all the pads," Botwood told him. "I'm putting them in and I'm typing it up because that's the only thing I can do."

"Show me," Hollis told him. Aghast at how slow the manual process appeared to be going, he said: "Oh my god, I asked you to do *this*?"

"Yes, this is what you asked me to do," Botwood replied. "Manually join the dots throughout all the levels."

Hollis walked out of Botwood's office and set to work on a converter that massively sped up Botwood's process, allowing him to finish in another two weeks what would have taken three or four months to do by hand. "That's the first time somebody made a video game tool specifically for me," Botwood told me, and it blew his mind.

The team worked this closely throughout the development process, collaborating every step of the way—particularly during the level setup period, when *GoldenEye* transformed from a set of tools and architecture into an actual game.

When Doak first joined the team at the end of 1995, *GoldenEye*'s levels were just barebones architecture—no objectives, enemies, or plot. After designing the watch menu, he and Botwood started creating a single-player campaign that followed and expanded upon *GoldenEye* the movie's narrative—a difficult task, considering the fact that the film's dialogue about Lienz Cossack traitors and Kyrgyz missile tests went over the heads of quite a few twelve-year-olds. Doak and Botwood's job was to tell this complicated story using rudimentary pre- and post-mission cutscenes, pre-mission briefing paperwork, in-game conversations with NPCs, and mission objectives, which proved the most powerful way to allow players to experience the story themselves.

The biggest inspiration for *GoldenEye*'s objective design was not another first-person shooter but rather *Super Mario 64*. "I studiously tried to learn what Nintendo was," Hollis said in 2015 of his years at Rare. "I played *Link to the Past* from beginning to end—I got all the hearts and all but two of the quarter hearts. I could write a thousand pages about that game. Then [an early version of] *Mario 64* came out during the development of *GoldenEye* and we were clearly influenced by that game. Ours was much more open as a result." Hollis took from *Super Mario 64* the idea of including multiple mission objectives within one level, just as the player can return to levels in *Super Mario 64* to collect new stars. For instance, in the Control level, the player must protect Natalya, disable the GoldenEye satellite, and destroy some armored mainframes.

GoldenEye's mission objectives add variety to what a player has to do beyond just shooting people and blowing stuff up. Sometimes you have to rescue hostages or steal secret documents, and other times you have to disarm bombs or sneakily infiltrate a base. The game's instruction manual makes clear how differently *GoldenEye* treats its objectives from other games of the time: "Unlike other first-person perspective games," it reads, "the object of the game isn't necessarily to destroy everything or everyone you come into contact with. Some people or objects are necessary to complete the mission. Shoot the wrong person or destroy the wrong computer and the mission could be a failure. Make sure to read through the list of objectives for each mission. The fate of the free world depends on it!"

Emotional drama in games is best structured by carefully tuning the highs and the lows like a roller coaster, with brief lulls after big periods of action. Doak and Botwood established a rhythm to the missions so that fast, action-packed levels like Dam and Runway were followed by quieter, stealthier levels like Facility and Surface, respectively. To vary each level's pace, the two designers brainstormed a large variety of creative objectives. For instance, instead of just collecting keys—the already well-established formula for first-person shooters that id Software had established in

Wolfenstein and *Doom*—in *GoldenEye,* the player makes use of more interesting, Bondian riffs on finding keys such as shooting a lock off a door or rendezvousing with an undercover agent to receive a door decoder. The level designers even tried objectives that wound up being technically infeasible. For instance, they originally wanted players to ride a motorbike through the Runway level, chasing the plane down the runway just like in the original movie. When this proved too difficult to pull off, the motorbike was repurposed as a miniature model on a desk in one of the Surface level's cabins.

The motorbike wasn't the only thing the developers couldn't fit in. The team originally wanted to include another level between the Jungle and Control missions called "Perimeter," but the level never made it past the earliest blocking stages. Another level cut from the game was a Casino mission in keeping with the movie—in fact, the game's ROM still includes money, a casino token, and a gold bar. In the end, Botwood said later, "there would have been such a lot of work to make a good casino background that we decided against it."

In the Streets level, the team originally intended for the player to chase the evil General Ourumov through the streets of St. Petersburg, just like in the movie, and they even modeled Bond's BMW Roadster and Ourumov's ZIL car from the film. But after this proved impossible, the workaround they settled on was having Bond navigate a tank through streets full of mines, patrolled by guards with grenades and grenade launchers. During our interview, Doak showed me a hand-drawn map of Streets from the development era. "My god, this is an absolute embarrassment because it's just shonkily thrown together," Doak chuckled. "In the film it's an amazing, stunt-laden scene. But then we came up with the idea that the tank could squish people and that's funny. We always joked about the tank—it's like Bond's made himself into a giant car," due to the way the first-person perspective doesn't change at all when you're using the tank.

The most famous of *GoldenEye*'s scrapped design elements remains visible to players. The Dam mission is home to one of the game's most tantalizing mysteries—a distant island viewable through the sniper rifle's scope, impossible to get to but so seemingly intentional that it left a generation of gamers wondering. Botwood and Edmonds said they had originally been planning to add a boat that would allow you to get to the island to complete a mission objective.

"If I did it today I'd probably have a control for an open water outlet pipe that was blocking Bond's [bungee] jump there, so you'd have to go there to turn off the water," Botwood speculated later. "I think the original plan was to have a building over there to go and investigate, with armour as a reward. That would have meant a boat ride needed to be coded in, and some of the scenery had gaps when viewed from the island, so it was too much work." Late in development, it was way more difficult to take something like the island out than to just leave it in, Hilton told me.

Looking back on it now, Botwood considers the island a mistake. "I should have never put it there," he told me. "It's a visual annoyance." But messy things like the island add to *GoldenEye*'s mythology—they add life to the world and give players something to theorize about, and are some of the best examples of the hand-crafted quality of the game.

For Double Fine content and community manager Harper Jay MacIntyre, the Dam signifies the kind of implicit promise of 3D spaces in the late 90s. "Shifting from 2D to 3D, the worlds [felt] so much bigger," MacIntyre told me. "*GoldenEye* levels are pretty short, but the first time you were playing those, especially back then, it's easy to get lost, and it's really intoxicating to think that there are secrets waiting for you." Even—or perhaps especially—if you can't ever reach them.

•

Every kid who's ever wanted to be a game developer when they grow up fantasizes about having a job playing video games all day. And while that's mostly a wildly inaccurate conception of the job, it's exactly how Doak and Botwood designed *GoldenEye*. Because the game ran playably throughout development, the team could playtest, riff, and iterate all throughout the level setup period—a process Doak attributes to the game's success.

"If I have one thing to say about making games, it's that [iteration is] the way to make games," Doak said in 2017, "and anyone who tells you otherwise is wrong. Yes, you can plan things, but the real magic happens when you have something which works and runs and you just iterate the hell out of it."

"It was a game that broke all the rules in the way we made it," Hilton told me, "because we had very little in the way of design documentation, we had no proof of concept or project management or planning going on. There was no thought really about the budget—it was just made by a bunch of people in a barn who were really enthusiastic about it."

The small size of the team allowed their process to unfold organically. The developers enjoyed a tight coupling between feature requests, coding, and bug-fixing, but only because the game designer sat one cubicle away from the artist and the programmer. When Doak showed me his hand-drawn map of Streets, he pointed out that it was marked up in two different people's handwriting—Hilton's rendering specs and Doak's notes on guard routes. When Doak needed to change things in the code, he had to manually type them into Hilton's computer, which ran the editing software. "It didn't have the automatic pipeline," Doak told me, so there was "a real possibility for mistyping stuff and it causing chaos somewhere else."

Still, this extreme collaboration meant that Hilton could, for instance, make precise, immediate changes to levels based on Doak's requests—adding a door or a room only took about a half a day's work. "Most of the game design decisions we made came out of discussions between two or more people," Botwood told me. He added that *GoldenEye* was the most collaborative project he's ever worked on, with each team member taking on multiple roles, since Hollis believed that defining team member roles too strictly hampered collaborative creativity. "It was the closest thing to an indie game I have ever worked on despite the license, despite the hardware support, despite the massive testing network," Botwood told me.

The team's process working on a AAA title in the mid-90s couldn't be more different from today. Norgate pointed out to me that with contemporary giant development teams, he can spend a whole day just trying to track someone down to ask them a question, which makes development more of a management challenge than a creative one. *GoldenEye*, on the other hand, "was done very much on a 'feel' basis with the whole team playing the game continually as it was developed and trying to make something we all enjoyed," Hilton said later.

"The right way to make a game is to make a prototype and test out your ideas," Hollis has said, "then make another version—an iterative, experimental process where it benefits you to admit you don't know what you're doing."

Hollis has spent years discussing the team's process. "I like [the design process] to be undefined," he told Game

Developer. Hollis values rough edges over polished final production values, and the team never felt "enslaved" to a formal design document or plan—in fact, less than a quarter of the way through development, Hollis stopped looking at his own game design document altogether, and Doak never even saw it until 2015.

"There wasn't some big grand design that everyone had to strictly follow," Doak said later. "If there was an idea that someone had, and it was convenient to do, we ran with it. We would build things and play it, and look for problems."

"We set out with an unusual attitude which was simply that we'd just model the graphics and not even think about whether it was possible to put them on the system—partly borne out of practical considerations because we didn't have any system," Hollis explained.

The team's lack of game design experience meant that they fell back on iterative design as their default method: "At the time I had zero experience of making video games so that's how I assumed things were done," Botwood noted in 2008. "My overwhelming memory of the development is one of everyone mucking in and helping each other, of pride in what we had made, and in utter surprise at the level of success that we achieved afterwards."

The young, inexperienced team felt "like a mini-company inside Rare making an atypical game that no one really thought was going to be any good," Doak said later. "The general feeling was that we were a bunch of students wasting time."

"I can't believe the Stampers just trusted a bunch of kids to make a game for such a huge license," Norgate told me. "It was still kind of the Wild West of video game development."

Still, the team's enthusiasm and ambition meant they'd try anything, as they had no sense of what wouldn't work. "Probably because none of us had done a game before," Hilton said in 1997, "we didn't worry too much about whether you could do this or not, or whether it had been done—we just thought: that would be a cool idea and that would be a cool idea, and we put it all in and when we finally got the stuff running we could see whether it was going to [work] or not."

This "joyful naïveté," as Doak has called it allowed the team to subvert generic conventions and invent entirely new ones.

"We were all flying by the seat of our pants," Kirkhope told me. "I think it's really freeing that way. If you don't know what the barriers are, you can just break through them."

The Stampers intentionally hired employees without prior experience in game development for this very reason. Fresh new staff brought complete enthusiasm about making cutting-edge, innovative games, and no preconceptions about what a game had to be. "No one had really worked on games before," Norgate told me, "not in the commercial sense, which was great because you didn't get people who were jaded or broken by it already."

The best example of how the team's inexperience benefited the final product is in their "backwards" or "anti" game design process. Today, much of the advice on FPS design says to start with objectives and work backward from there—tailor your level spaces to your objectives instead of building level architecture with no idea what will happen within that architecture.

Instead, the team designed *GoldenEye* backwards—levels first and objectives second. When Hilton created the level spaces, he paid little to no attention to the player's starting place, exit point, mission objectives, or enemy location. All of that came later, with Doak and Botwood's work.

"The benefit of this sloppy, unplanned approach was that many of the levels in the game have a realistic and non-linear feel," Hollis has said. "There are rooms with no direct relevance to the level. There are multiple routes across the level. This is an anti-game design approach, frankly. It is inefficient because much of the level is unnecessary to the gameplay. But it contributes to a greater sense of freedom, and also realism. And in turn this sense of freedom and realism contributed enormously to the success of the game."

It also helped the game succeed despite being a licensed game. Licensed games usually fail because they're rushed projects relying entirely on a movie's brand-name recognition. But games based on movies also often don't work for an even deeper reason: Films and games are fundamentally different media, involving very different forms of narrative immersion. Many licensed games fail because they focus too much on the source material's story rather than on the gameplay. Players must participate in the game world through immersive mechanics and lots of control, which is the opposite of sitting passively and watching a film. Games that have original stories usually fare better—they might expand an existing universe, like some Star Wars games, but don't feel beholden to telling a certain story a certain way.

At their core, games are more about place and space than story. When licensed games work, they do so by opening the worlds of film and television narratives for players to explore, rather than slavishly reproducing them. Films move fast and often fly through world-building, whereas in games players can explore all the little details of the film's spaces. *GoldenEye*'s open level design based on exact blueprints and photos of the film sets allows players to explore the spaces of the film, without feeling rushed by the film's need to constantly advance the story. Players can play as any kind of Bond they want to. Your Bond can be stealthy, fast, methodical, or an all-out murder machine. *You* tell the story. And with its varied mission objectives that go beyond the film's plot, *GoldenEye* lets you into an expanded version of the movie that you control, and the N64 technology allowed that to happen in 3D environments for the very first time.

•

One of the tensest moments in *GoldenEye* occurs in the game's penultimate level, Control, in a vast satellite control room full of tables with computers on them, all surrounded by balconies and sets of stairs. As Natalya types away on one of the computer terminals, hacking into the GoldenEye satellite to prevent it from firing on London, swarms of enemy guards begin pouring in from all sides, ruthlessly targeting her. You must protect Natalya from all these bad guys, picking each one off until she finishes her hacking mission.

"James, do you think you could be a bit quieter?" Natalya quips during the bombardment. "I can't hear myself think." She'll scream in pain if she's hit, and if she dies, you automatically lose the mission. But if you protect her long enough, she'll finally blurt out, "Did it! The satellite's orbit is decaying," then run out of the room to meet you later on in the game's final credits.

It's an exhilarating scene, with the story told entirely in the gameplay and not a cutscene to be found. And without an innovative approach to non-player-character (NPC) AI, none of it would have been possible.

One of Doak's biggest tasks during the level setup process was creating NPC AI behaviors that progressed the game's narrative and responded to player behavior. *GoldenEye*'s NPC AI was remarkably ahead of its time. Enemies react to you in seemingly realistic ways, like setting up ambush points, throwing grenades, and running to sound an alarm. Guards sometimes take bathroom breaks, and swat at flies as they stand at their post. Civilians flee in fear. Scientists put up their hands and tremble if you poke them with a gun. Friendly AI also behave in interesting ways—you can talk with them as part of the story, like meeting Valentin in a shady storage container, and watch them act out in-game cutscenes, like Ourumov shooting Trevelyan. Cooperative AI characters hand you objects, protect you on certain missions, and demand escort protection on other missions.

This was all pretty mind-blowing for a console game in 1997, especially considering the N64's limited memory, and it left a huge impact on future games like *Half-Life 2*, *Halo 3*, *Resident Evil 4*, *The Last of Us*, and many more. "It was the beginnings of having interesting non-combat AI in first-person games," Doak told the *Arcade Attack* podcast in 2020, "but we wouldn't have attempted it if we weren't trying to tell the [film's] story."

Early on in the development process, Hollis and Edmonds created a basic system for simple AI behavior: guards could attack the player and set off alarms, but not much else. As Doak started setting up levels, he worked with Edmonds to refine the AI to do more sophisticated things, like Natalya protecting Bond in the Jungle mission and Ourumov pretending to execute Trevelyan in the gas plant.

"But they don't know how to shoot each other," Edmonds would initially respond to Doak's request. "They don't even know each other exist."

"But it's in the film, and we kind of need to have it," Doak would tell him. And then Edmonds would disappear for a while and come back with a solution. "Nothing was impossible for him," Doak told me.

"From my point of view, Dave would come along and ask me to do something impossible," Edmonds told me in a separate interview, laughing. "There's always a way of doing anything you want to do—it's just a question of finding what will work," he added.

To implement Doak's vision, Edmonds created a virtual scripting language with a low-level machine code—atomic lists of individual commands for everything the NPC's and enemies needed to do. For instance:

```
// aiKneel()

// *****aiLookAtBond()     Look towards bond
                           then return to
                           stand

// aiSurprisedByBond()     Act surprised by
                           seeing bond

// aiOpenDoor(special)     Open the door
                           (even if locked)
```

The developers could then build sequences of more complicated AI behavior by linking up strings of these individual actions. In essence, the system acted as a basic finite state machine, in which something that occurs in the game triggers a certain behavior in the AI, changing its state and potentially setting off more reactions in the process. Edmonds's simple programming language took up less memory than it would have to code these responses in C.

Despite the innovation put into the technical approach to *GoldenEye*'s AI, when Hollis looks back on it, he sees it as "not all that intelligent." "There's a guard," he explained at a 2004 European Developers Forum talk. "He'd see you. Either he'd attack you, or maybe run to activate an alarm. Some had patrol routes, some didn't, just stood still. It was revolutionary for the time, but still not very clever." Hollis emphasizes that what made *GoldenEye*'s AI so great wasn't the AI technology itself but rather how the team incorporated it, which made it *feel* smarter. "There's no point having sophisticated AI that the player doesn't notice," Hollis explained. "Your NPCs can be insightfully discussing the meaning of life, but the player won't notice if the game requires that they swing around a corner and fill the bad guys with bullets. So the intelligence has to be evident. The game mechanics have to showcase the AI. The level setup has to showcase the AI. And it all has to make an actual difference in actual gameplay."

GoldenEye's guard patrols incentivize that players approach levels strategically to avoid passing into the line of sight of a guard—each of whom might react differently when they see you. At the beginning of the first Bunker level, for instance, when Bond enters the room, one guard runs for an alarm while the other begins attacking him. "Bond faces a dilemma: who to shoot first?" Hollis explained at the 2004 talk. "This scene, taken pretty much directly from one of the earlier screenplays of the movie was one of the most exciting scenes for me, in terms of gameplay and AI innovation. I'd never seen anything like it in a game. Consequently, alarms and people running to them was a major part of the AI of the game. But the times when this cleverness on the part of the programmers and designers really counted, was when you could see the NPC deciding what to do, and doing it. That is to say, when it is showcased."

Other features that emphasize the AI include civilians who flee from Bond or surrender, as well as the location-based hit animations that Botwood worked so hard to motion-capture. These hit animations significantly impact how players perceive the enemy's intelligence because they're the most immediate apparent AI response, indicating whether you nailed a headshot or nicked someone in the hand, for instance. "Sometimes, they seemed to be really thinking for themselves," an anonymous *GoldenEye* designer said in 2001. "You'd be playing and they'd catch you out with something really intelligent. You'd think, we didn't program them to do that."

At the time *GoldenEye* came out, no other game featured AI in quite this combination of ways. *Doom*'s monsters didn't have the same level of variety in their behaviors and choices, and *Turok*'s enemy AI mostly just stood still and shot at you. *GoldenEye*'s AI, on the other hand, forced players to make strategic decisions playing more aggressively or more stealthily and deciding how to prioritize threats, including security cameras and alarms that needed to be destroyed to cover Bond's tracks.

"At the start of *GoldenEye*, sneaking wasn't really one of the core gameplay mechanics," Doak told Nintendo Life in 2020, "apart from the fact you might set off alarms. It just became a gameplay mechanic as we started to flesh out the level and found that it worked."

The world's most famous spy was, of course, the perfect IP to match with this technical innovation, allowing the game to "portra[y] the odds against one man in a slightly more realistic manner," an anonymous team member told *NGC Magazine*. "Players who wanted to approach games in a stealthy way were given a proper outlet for the first time."

In addition to a visual testing system involving a polygonal mesh with navigation markers, Hollis and Edmonds created a clever audio detection system to encourage stealth gameplay. Audio sensors ran proximity checks based on the type of weapon and rate of fire as well as the distance to a certain guard's radius. "The game would count how many shots you fired," Hollis explained later. "Two shots from the PPK was considered 'silent.' Two shots from the [KF7 Soviet] was considered 'loud' and guards nearby would become alarmed, and would know where you were. If you didn't shoot for a few seconds, the count would be reset. Not very realistic. But very effective at balancing stealthy play. It encouraged single-shot use of the weapons, which in turn encouraged accuracy. This worked well together with the single head-shot kills rule. But all this encouraged strategy, as you could choose a method to play a level, and you would benefit from thinking before shooting every time. Encouraging strategy was one more reason for the success of the game."

Perhaps no level exemplifies this better than Archives, in which you start out under arrest in a small interrogation room with two guards. Taking these guys out isn't the problem (there's a gun and ammo lying on the table in front of you) so much as escaping the room afterwards, when guards swarm in and corner you. No matter how many guards you take out, it seems like they never stop coming.

That's because they never will. In certain missions, the game punishes loud gunfire with endlessly generating guards. NPCs only activate their AI behavior if they've been rendered, so if an NPC hears a sound but hasn't been drawn yet (for instance, if a guard in another room hears you), a clone of that guard spawns and runs over to check out the commotion. The clones won't stop spawning until the loud gunfire stops, which means that no matter how many of the Archives guards you gun down in the interrogation room, you will never be able to kill them all. The only surefire way to survive the interrogation room is to avoid using your gun entirely and quietly karate chop your way out instead—the game's way of encouraging stealth and strategy.

One of Hollis's favorite memories as a player of *GoldenEye* took advantage of this infinite spawning effect. "[*GoldenEye* is] not really a sandbox game," Hollis explained, "but there's a sandbox-y way to play it, and that's when you don't care about the missions anymore— when you've played it enough and you just want to mess around with the guys. My personal favorite [is that] I spent six hours one evening playing and playing in the Bunker, drawing in more of the infinite spawn enemies and shooting their hats off […] I had a massive collection of hats on the ground" to juggle in the air by shooting them. "That is a really pleasurable thing and it came out of the game development totally organically."

•

One fateful day during the level setup process, Doak inserted a character into *GoldenEye* who would eventually become legendary. He added to the game's second level, Facility, a scientist double agent with whom the player must meet up to complete the level. Partly as a placeholder and partly as a joke for the rest of the team, he gave the scientist his face, using Jones's photographs of all the team members, and named him "Dr. Doak." He always expected the character's name would eventually be changed, since the Stamper brothers weren't keen on highlighting individuals over the monolithic company brand. Putting an employee's name visibly in the game was a big no-no.

But Tim Stamper's eventual demand to have Dr. Doak removed from the game annoyed Hollis, who "didn't like having edicts placed on him," Doak said later. It annoyed Hollis so much that he waited until localization, when it would be too hard to make any more changes, and then snuck Dr. Doak back in.

"I think they said we should call him Dr. Dust or something like that, but we stuck to our guns because Dave was an actual doctor," Botwood said later.

"We were a bit like naughty schoolboys with management," Doak explained in 2019.

Once Dr. Doak returned to the game for good, Rare apparently leaned into the joke. The "cast list" of the *GoldenEye* page on Rare's late-90s website lists Bond, Trevelyan, Natalya, Xenia, and other major characters from the film and game, with a bio and headshot for each. At the bottom is a headshot of the real-life David Doak with the bio: "Oxford-educated biochemist and double agent. Knows where to get secret door decoder things from, which is why he got one; also knows exactly when to get out of the Facility. Never fully explained whether he speaks Russian." Now, Doak enjoys having his name so intimately connected with the game. "It is a source of deep joy to be associated with the game in that way," he said in a recent Reddit Ask Me Anything. "I love being Dr Doak. Particularly when people tell me they have shot me so many times…"

Dr. Doak isn't the only cameo in the game—not by a long shot. In addition to the team members' faces appearing on guards, they pop up frequently in subtler places as well. For instance, the gates into Statue Park say "BJ" on them, Doak told me, not for "Bond, James," as some have speculated, but for "Brett Jones." And more visual cameos abound: an image of Botwood appears on the side of a wall in Statue Park, and the Russian general ranting on the computer screens in Bunker is Doak again, dressed up in sunglasses and a Russian hat Hilton had bought in Berlin. The most elusive presence in the game is Edmonds, a private person who preferred not to appear too recognizably, which was a relief, Jones noted, because his curly hair would have been too difficult to model without a lot of pixels. "What I did do was I managed to get a shot of him walking," Jones said later, "and if you look on one of the screens in [the bunker], you will see a guy with a hat on a skateboard just doing the skateboard motion over and over and over again, and this is Mark Edmonds."

GoldenEye was made by playful jokesters in a serious workplace environment—by young, inexperienced rookies who cared a great deal about the quality of their work. It's this tension that created the game we know and love today: a quirky, goofy, finely tuned work of art. A game as precisely crafted as it is fun to play, with the faces of its perfectionist naughty schoolboy creators etched literally onto the walls and characters and computer screens of every level.

FROM TWYCROSS
WITH LOVE

ON A WARM SUMMER NIGHT late in the development process, Doak and Hollis were playing the Caverns level with the soundtrack to the movie *Heat* blasting out of Hollis's huge speakers and the barn windows open. Their favorite song, "Force Marker," was a driving, suspenseful percussive track used during an intense shootout chase scene in the classic De Niro/Pacino heist film. The sound perfectly evoked the feeling they wanted to create for Caverns, in which the player chases the villain Alec Trevelyan through corridors and shoots at him with high-powered weapons just like the ones in *Heat*.

At around 10 p.m., Chris Stamper, who must have heard the loud, thumping music and explosive gunfire effects, stepped into the barn to see what was going on. Stamper believed so strongly in a hyper-focused work environment that he banned headphones from the office, at least until 5 p.m. After that point, the mood around Rare changed a lot.

"How can you guys work with all that noise?" Stamper asked the young men.

"Actually, the music is kind of part of it," Doak and Hollis told him, attempting, perhaps futilely, to explain how they were going about embedding into their game the true ethos of an action movie. Even 25 years later, "I just have a complete mental picture of that evening," Doak told me.

It took a long time to get to the point when the game felt fun enough to play. In fact, Hollis later said it took two years to finish even one decent level. Doak has said that most games are awful for about 80 percent of the process—there's no fun in the game until the very end. Now that *GoldenEye* had started feeling fun, the team spent the last year trying to finish it as quickly as possible after having missed several initial deadlines already. So much time had passed since *GoldenEye* the movie premiered that *Tomorrow Never Dies*, the next Bond movie, was almost due out—in the end, it premiered only a few months after the game. "The last year of development we were always trying to finish the game as soon as we could, but the date would get pushed a little bit, then pushed a little bit more, so we kept tinkering and adding new things," Doak said in 2018.

At one point, Tim Stamper called the team in for a pep talk. "You know, this is kind of important," Stamper told them. "It's not like some student project where it doesn't matter whether you get it done or not." Although Stamper didn't mention it, missing deadline after deadline had real consequences—the team just never knew about them. For three months, Nintendo stopped funding the project entirely because of all its bugs and delays, but Rare kept paying the team to work on it and didn't tell them about the pressure from Nintendo. "The management at Rare were very supportive of the team during development, and shielded us from a lot of that," Botwood said later.

In interview after interview, members of the Bond team have recalled that, apart from Tim's pep talk, they heard very little pressure from management around deadlines. Rare had complete faith in its employees, and wanted them to focus on making the best game they could. And so they protected the team's creative freedom and insulated them from any pressure, not even asking for progress reports. "We really got left alone to make the best thing we possibly could," Kirkhope told me.

But as patient as Rare was, *GoldenEye* was still, in Hollis's words, "awfully, tragically, disastrously late," and they worked around the clock to complete the game. "In this final year, we were working so hard, I can't remember it at all," Hollis said in 2012. The *GoldenEye* pressure got to one *GoldenEye* team member so bad that he ended up leaving Rare in February 1997. Ady Smith visited the hospital twice for a stress-related panic attack while working on *Donkey Kong Country 2*, and his work got no less stressful when he joined the *GoldenEye* team. "Working 15 to 17 hours a day and working weekends does in the end catch up with you at some point," he told *Arcade Attack*. "I nearly suffered another attack and I would not wish that on anyone. A culmination of these two things led to me resigning from Rare. No job is worth your health."

•

Meanwhile, the N64's release in North America was going terribly. Even after Sega had given them a run for their money during the 16-bit era's console wars, Nintendo remained extremely overconfident about the supremacy of the N64. An ad for the console bragged: "It's the best thing I've ever seen. —God." Nintendo was about to face a harsh awakening.

The company had announced it would release the N64 in time for Christmas 1995, but missed that deadline by almost a year in North America and by even more in Europe and Australia. The delay let Sony and Sega take hold of the market with the PlayStation and Saturn, respectively, as retailers, gamers, and press all grew frustrated with the N64's constant delays. After they missed their April 1996 deadline and then their June 1996 deadline, Nintendo leaned in and organized a marketing campaign around the delays with an advertising blitz totaling $100 million. The general strategy was "FUD": create enough fear, uncertainty, and doubt that consumers would wait to choose their next console purchase until after the N64 launched. The ads said things like: "About to buy a new games machine? Is it worth waiting? Yes. [...] You can't buy [the N64] yet. After all, nothing this good comes easy. But do you really want something less powerful? WAIT FOR IT..." Many customers did. Yet even after all the long wait, when the console finally did ship in North America in September 1996, the only games available for it were *Super Mario 64* and *Pilotwings 64.*

Still, due to the long wait and heightened expectations, Nintendo sold 350,000 of its 500,000 available consoles just three days after launch. In just its first week out, the N64 sold as many consoles as all its competitors for the entire month of September, and four months after its release, the N64 had sold more than the PlayStation did in its entire first year. Kids like me who grew up devoted to the NES and SNES had their minds completely blown by the N64's true 3D gameplay, and critics doted on the machine. The N64's state-of-the-art graphical processing power—two to four times that of the PlayStation—allowed it to render complex 3D environments and dazzling graphics at such a fast speed that it made Sega and Sony's disc-based 32-bit consoles seem sluggish in comparison. With four controller ports, the later addition of the Rumble Pak, and the revolutionary joystick controller, the N64 was technologically superior to any other console of its time.

But a few months after its release, N64 sales started to slow down because no one was making games for it. Sony had gone out of its way to make developing software for the PlayStation easier, whereas programming for the N64 was annoyingly complex. Plus, the N64 seemed outdated to many developers because it used cartridges while its competitors all used discs. "It was both a very modern and an antiquated console at the same time," N64 Today founder Martin Watts told me.

It didn't help that third-party developers were tiring of Nintendo's strict licensing rules and punishing royalty policies. The company's decision to stick with more expensive and risky cartridges finally pushed some developers over the edge. Square, for instance, defected to Sony for *Final Fantasy VII* after Nintendo opted for cartridges. As third-party developers abandoned Nintendo, they created a huge games library for Sony. The N64 just didn't have enough games to drive console sales—an issue that had killed previous consoles like the Atari 7800 and the Atari Jaguar. By the end of 1997, the N64 offered fewer than 50 games compared to the PlayStation's thousand. This gap eventually widened in the end to about 400 total N64 games compared to 4,400 PlayStation titles.

While Sony focused on gaining a ton of licenses for their games from hot names like *Top Gun*, Spiderman, Batman, Looney Tunes, the NBA, the NHL, and NASCAR, Nintendo opted for a smaller stable of top-notch developer partners like Rare, desperately clinging onto their mantra that the quality of their games mattered more than quantity. "Software is what sells hardware," Nintendo of America chairman Howard Lincoln said in 1994. "We're convinced that a few great games at [the N64's] launch are more important than great games mixed in with a lot of dogs." To guarantee this level of quality in their N64 titles, Nintendo had created an elite "Dream Team" of third-party publishers and developers that included Paradigm, Angel, LucasArts, and, of course, Rare—Chris and Tim Stamper stayed loyal to Nintendo even as other developers jumped ship.

Nevertheless, the lack of games for the N64 ultimately cost Nintendo its long-held commanding position in console sales. Worldwide, Nintendo sold around 33 million N64 consoles over the course of its retail lifetime, while Sony sold more than three times as many PlayStations at 124.9 million. The N64 and its successor the GameCube marked Nintendo's biggest slumps in home console sales until the Wii U in 2012, which sold only 13.56 million units worldwide due in part to the same problem—a lack of games.

The N64's sales woes meant that Sony emerged from the era as a new console leader, targeting gamers over twenty while Sega and Nintendo fought over kids with Sonic and Mario. The question is: How much worse off would Nintendo's situation have been without Rare? Without *GoldenEye*? Rare certainly earned its position on Nintendo's "Dream Team," producing six of the twenty best-selling N64 games. "The stuff Rare did, particularly [on] the N64, kept Nintendo in business," Doak told Eurogamer. "It was a powerhouse. Without the Rare catalogue, Nintendo might not be in business now." Because the N64 sold better in America than in Japan, Nintendo relied upon Rare's ability to produce games with an American aesthetic, and (ironically, since Bond is British) nothing was more American than an action movie full of guns. Did *GoldenEye* help save the N64 from complete and utter failure?

One in four N64 owners owned *GoldenEye*, and while it's impossible to know how many of those customers bought an N64 just to play *GoldenEye*, we can certainly speculate. It's telling, for instance, that Nintendo released two different versions of the N64 console bundled with the *GoldenEye* cartridge, one of which even featured a limited-edition gold controller. (Between 5,000 and 10,000 of these were released, according to one online console database). Scholars and games journalists alike have dubbed *GoldenEye* the N64's killer app that drove sales of the console by injecting a new spark of life into the device for the Christmas 1997 sales season.

Furthermore, in the mid-90s, Nintendo desperately needed to seem relevant to older gamers, especially after Sega had trashed their kid-friendly image during the console wars. In response, the company began experimenting with more mature titles like *GoldenEye* and the brash Rare title *Conker's Bad Fur Day* (2001), which they advertised in *Maxim*, on Comedy Central's *The Man Show*, and even on a line of bar coasters. Just as the public had started to view the N64 as a toy rather than an adult entertainment device, *GoldenEye* proved that the console supported more mature, sophisticated titles for older gamers. Reviewers at the time called *GoldenEye* "the game that causes little green lights to appear in the eyes of PC and

PlayStation owners" and "a sore subject for PlayStation owners." One reviewer went so far as to claim that "If more N64 games use [*GoldenEye*] as a model […] then perhaps the system really does have a shot at toppling the PlayStation's reign as the dominant game platform."

Finally, open-world games like *Super Mario 64* and *GoldenEye* played to the N64's strengths, making the most out of the console's incredible 3D graphics technology. In fact, Watts argues that while the N64 wasn't as successful as other consoles of the era in terms of sales, it left its impact in the form of genre-defining games like *Super Mario 64* and *GoldenEye*, which revolutionized not just platformers and shooters but all games, particularly for how well the games made use of 3D technology. "[*GoldenEye*] offered a level of freedom that we hadn't had in video games," Watts told me, with both level design and the joystick controller offering new ways to explore bigger game environments.

GoldenEye helped keep the N64 afloat even if it was also a deviation in Nintendo's otherwise kid-focused, cartoony games library. And in this way, it was the game that marked a transition point in the industry from marketing consoles as kids' toys to eventually marketing them as adult-oriented *Halo* machines.

•

In this last year of development, after *GoldenEye* had reached the testing stage, the team worked to fine-tune difficulty settings and to create ways to introduce players to the gameplay. *GoldenEye*'s very first level, Dam, exemplifies how the team approached both of these challenges. The level kicks the game off with action and style, just like the opening sequence of any Bond movie. Your mission is to navigate your way through the different gates and outbuildings into a heavily guarded Soviet chemical weapons facility, past several guard towers and along the top of the dam, to a platform from which you bungee jump down into the facility's ventilation system. Dam throws you into the action right away, equipping you with Bond's trusty silenced PP7 but also introducing you to the sniper rifle, which in turn teaches players the joys of headshots and aiming thanks to the intentionally spaced guard towers along the top of the dam.

Dam basically acts as a tutorial for the whole game, with no patronizing onscreen instructions but rather an intuitive playground in which to learn the game's core mechanics. You can beat Dam by slinking around stealthily or by running and gunning. You can choose from long and short-range guns, some loud and others quiet. You can pick off the guards in the tunnels carefully with your sniper rifle or flamboyantly blow up the explosive gasoline tanks around them. Dam introduces one of the greater joys of *GoldenEye*: all the many different ways to murder someone.

During testing, *GoldenEye* received excellent feedback from Rare's in-house testers and from Nintendo, with staffers putting in voluntary overtime just to test it. Nintendo of America chairman Howard Lincoln himself championed the title, one of the only games he ever actually played himself during testing. But one piece of playtesting feedback resulted in an important change. Doak's initial level setups included around five objectives per level, and in early playtesting, players kept failing early missions because they couldn't figure out all the objectives while learning the level layout for the first time. The solution to this problem resulted in *GoldenEye*'s difficulty settings, in which each higher difficulty level ("Agent," the slightly harder "Secret Agent," then the very hard "00 Agent") required the player to complete more objectives. "What happened was that we made 00 Agent and then we stripped things out to make the easier ones," Doak told me, as opposed to *adding* more objectives for each new difficulty level, which is how most people assume the team's process went.

Even after adjusting the difficulty settings, *GoldenEye* remained a challenging game. "This kind of difficulty would be pretty much unacceptable" today, Doak noted later. *GoldenEye*'s missions didn't offer any checkpoints or health pickups, as in today's games, and little to no body armor in 00 Agent mode. But the decision to add more objectives to higher difficulty levels significantly increased *GoldenEye*'s replayability and added more meaningful difficulty to the game.

"I always liked the idea of different difficulties, but I really wanted them to actually *do* something, other than just be harder, more enemy types, different level design (as possible with the old tech), unlocks, different endings, whatever," Lobb said in 2012.

Adjusting a game's difficulty level can be a tough balancing act for a developer, because increasing the amount of damage a player suffers may scare the player off from taking interesting risks. But as *GoldenEye* difficulty's increased, you're forced to complete more objectives and therefore keep taking risks. The additional objectives also encourage more player exploration. In Dam, for instance, the only objective on Agent mode is to reach the bungee platform and escape the level, much like a platformer or *Doom.* But once you completed Agent difficulty, you might notice that you could play as a Secret Agent and take on additional new objectives, which happened to take place in the subterranean portion of the level that you might have overlooked on Agent mode. "You're having to explore after having learned it and played it, so the game is showing you something new," Botwood told me. "That gives you a lovely feeling of discovery as a player."

•

If one of the best feelings you can have playing *GoldenEye* is the sight of a guard crumbling to the ground after a perfectly placed headshot, then one of the worst is seeing red blood rain down on your screen after you've been killed in action. Both images proved controversial during *GoldenEye*'s testing period, when the game's level of violence was endlessly questioned and calibrated.

"It was very much in my mind that Bond does kill people, he does have a license to kill," Hollis noted in a Game Developers Conference talk. In 1997, however, Nintendo eschewed violence of any kind, letting its cartoon heroes like Mario, Link, and Donkey Kong bear the flag for their squeaky-clean, family-friendly brand. In fact, many N64 games were censored as they transitioned from arcade and PC to console. Nintendo's SNES port of *Mortal Kombat*, for instance, [in]famously transformed sprays of red blood into gray sweat.

In Japan in 1997, first-person shooters enjoyed nowhere near the popularity they had achieved in America, mainly due to differing cultural attitudes about violence. "The evolution of video games in the US cannot be extricated from warfare," author Jonathan Hennessey writes. "That was not the case, however, in Japan—where they went hand-in-hand with toys and entertainment. Perhaps the whimsical, psychedelic setting and play of [Super Mario Bros. games] arises not just from [Mario creator] Shigeru Miyamoto's acclaimed imagination but also the less bellicose nature of postwar Japan." With its strict gun laws and low military presence, Japan doesn't share the same cultural fascination with guns as America. Japanese games tend to adopt an anime style over hyper-realism, and while America fell in love with first-person shooters, Japanese gamers sought out RPGs like *Final Fantasy* and *Dragon Quest*. There's even a whole word in Japanese for "Western games" (aka first-person shooters) like *Call of Duty*: *yōgē* or 洋ゲ which literally translates to "games from across the ocean."

But the FPS genre was growing rapidly in the 90s, and Nintendo wanted to capitalize on that trend. "In the US, various types of FPS games made for PCs slowly began to be released on home consoles," legendary Nintendo designer and Mario creator Shigeru Miyamoto said in a Nintendo in-house interview. "However, in Japan, there had been no basis for FPS-style games, and advanced games just kind of sprung up suddenly. I think it was our responsibility to continue releasing fun FPS games to the public to keep them engaged and interested." And so Miyamoto himself began "proactively supporting such projects like [*GoldenEye 007*]," as he put it.

It helped, too, that Bond was big in Japan and generally more of a PG-13 than an R-rated film series. Hilton noted in 2018 that "What could have been construed as a violent first-person shooter was opened up to a much broader family audience because, culturally, James Bond is allowed to kill people and not be seen as bad. It meant children could ask parents for the game!"

Edmonds said in 2018 that *GoldenEye*'s sales depended on a "T" for "Teen" rating rather than an "M" for "Mature," and this took some tweaking to achieve, since *GoldenEye*'s graphics were much gorier at first. At one point, the game included exploding chests and huge spatters of gushing blood.

"When I was doing the animation and I was testing it, I was making myself feel quite sick, because it looked quite gratuitous," Smith told me. "When I was doing the effects for the blood, we had two [RCP-90s] and when you were testing the hits in the firing range, it looked like you were cutting the characters in half with the blood effects that were going on, so it was a bit [over the top]."

The original gore art consisted of about 40 textures including "a fountain of blood, like that moment in *The Shining* when the lift doors open," Hollis said in 2015.

Before Nintendo ever saw the game, the team realized they needed to scale back the gore. They wanted the game's animations and modeling to look as realistic as possible, but the excessive gore was too comedic to match the game's tone. Hollis noted later that the team downplayed the shock value of headshots by eliminating "explosions of blood or gore" and dialed down the redness of the blood by 20 percent after experimenting with unrealistic green, orange, and bright blue blood that all looked terrible.

Still, *GoldenEye*'s level of violence upset Miyamoto himself so much that he faxed Hollis some personal suggestions along with concerns that the game was a "murder simulator" with too much "point-blank killing."

"He felt the game was too tragic, with all the killing," Hollis said later. "He suggested that it might be nice if, at the end of the game, you got to shake hands with all your enemies in the hospital." "It seems ridiculous," Hollis told *Retro Gamer*, "but you have to look deeper at feedback like that. It was all about the close-up killing. You could see the pain and suffering—they'd get down on their knees and then you'd shoot them again in the head. It felt personal. Unsurprisingly, this didn't sit well with Nintendo. I was trying to negotiate a line between being true to Bond and Nintendo's family-friendly brand."

Nintendo of America chairman Howard Lincoln hated *GoldenEye*'s violence so much—in particular, a long animation of a guard writhing around on the ground in agony after a shot to the groin—that Botwood believes it's the reason the company temporarily cancelled the game. After about a year and a half of development, Botwood remembers, Lincoln came to check on the game the day after they'd put in the obscene blood splatter effect, which Botwood compared to spraying a bottle of ketchup everywhere. "He didn't say anything" after viewing the demo, Botwood told me, and walked out of the barn in silence. "We didn't hear anything about that but he basically cancelled the project," Botwood told me, though the team never found out about this from the Stampers.

MGM staffers also had concerns about the number of people Bond murdered. Late in development, with the game close to the finish line, some MGM suits came to the barn to check in on the game and told the team they found the level of violence unacceptable. "When you shoot these guys, they look like they've been hurt," Doak remembers them saying. "Bond doesn't do that."

"They wanted a sanitised version of Bond who doesn't shoot anyone," Doak explained later. But "[i]f you go back to Sean Connery, he'd shoot people for a laugh. Smoke tabs, shoot people, shag birds."

In the end, the team worked in a few compromises. First, they made guard corpses disappear shortly after death. Partly this kept the game running at a decent speed by reducing the amount of visuals on screen, but it also "kind of underlines the fact that you shouldn't really care about [the dead enemies]," Hollis said in 2012. "That you shouldn't feel bad about shooting them—it makes it easier to play a game which is, like any first-person shooter, essentially about killing a long, long series of people." Hollis added that the game's blocky, non-realistic graphics also helped lighten up the mood of the game and keep it more in line with the Bond universe.

Hollis also addressed Miyamoto's concerns by reviving all the murdered characters at the end of the game and showcasing them in a credit sequence called "The Cast." This intended to make clear that the killing wasn't real but rather all part of a film with actors playing their parts—akin to the way Miyamoto ended *Super Mario Bros. 3* with a curtain call. "It was very filmic, and the key thing was, it underlined that this was artifice," Hollis said later.

The "minimize scientist casualty" objective, common on many missions, came out of Miyamoto's famous fax too, Doak told me. "It came later, but it's a great objective because it adds this cakewalk because there are all these scientists operating these highly explosive desks," Doak laughed. Indeed, scientists often run directly into ambient explosions, making the objective a tougher one to achieve than you might think.

Years later, Hollis agrees with Miyamoto's points. "When first reading [Miyamoto's] fax, a person might jump to the conclusion that Nintendo did not understand James Bond at all," Hollis told me. "However, with the benefit of hindsight, I can be definitive and say that Nintendo's advice was valuable indeed." Hollis said he tried to see past the exact words of the fax and find the "spirit" of the feedback. "The end result was that we used this paragraph of feedback about 'close violence' in various ways. One example was Dave Doak's idea to place the sniper rifle on the Dam. I think this was likely partly inspired by […] Mr. Miyamoto's feedback about distancing. You can't necessarily make a square into a circle, but you can round off the corners a little. And the sniper rifle appearing on the Dam does soften the violence on the first level, as well as being pure gold as game design by giving a strong sandbox dimension to the level." Murder in the close distance, meet murder in the far distance—which, in the case of the sniper rifle, was even more fun.

SLAPPERS ONLY

I'M SITTING ON THE FLOOR of my college dorm room shoulder to shoulder with my best friend, my boyfriend, and my boyfriend's best friend. We're sharing a bag of Doritos, talking, laughing, and shooting each other in the face. The TV screen we're all staring at is split into four quadrants—one for each of us—and we're stalking each other up and down the corrugated metal catwalks of *GoldenEye*'s Complex level in multiplayer mode, cackling at any opportunity to pin someone down in a corner and riddle them with Klobb bullets or blow them up from across the room with a rocket launcher.

I can't remember the first time I played *GoldenEye* the same way I can't remember the first time I played tag—it was always just there, an ever-present staple of my childhood and adolescence. A go-to social activity for any group of two or more people. *GoldenEye*'s multiplayer mode is what most nostalgic gamers remember best—it's the feature that elevated the game from bestseller to legend.

That's because while *GoldenEye* is fun to play in campaign mode, it really comes to life in multiplayer.

Even the team members themselves agree. In a 2018 interview, Edmonds said that "[t]he multiplayer contributed massively to the overall success, as you could just go on playing and playing and playing. And the friends you played with would then go and play the game with other friends, helping to spread its success."

Doak added in a separate interview: "It wouldn't have had the legs that it has had if it wasn't for the multiplayer."

At sleepovers and in college dorm rooms across the world, friends, roommates, and siblings bonded over toggle-able play modes like rocket launchers and "Slappers Only." Ask any Millennial gamer what they remember of *GoldenEye* and you'll hear a treasure trove of stories: that friend who camped body armor in Bunker and set mines at the spawn points in Facility, the cousin who insisted on playing as Oddjob, long sessions at friends' houses kept secret from disapproving parents, and always, always intensely fierce competition.

GoldenEye featured one of the first console-based first-person shooter multiplayer modes ever, and definitely the first good one. Although PC shooters at the time already had multiplayer modes, if you played console games only, then *GoldenEye* was likely your introduction to the multiplayer deathmatch. And so multiplayer mode didn't just make *GoldenEye* itself the wild critical, commercial, and cult classic success that it was—it also, in the words of *NME* journalist Mark Beaumont "helped to introduce gaming as a group event and helped pave the way for *Halo* and the eGaming explosion." Its influence on the entire gaming industry simply cannot be overstated.

But *GoldenEye*'s multiplayer mode almost never got made.

•

GoldenEye's multiplayer all started with a game cartridge getting hurled out of a window. The team blew off steam during their long days at the office by playing networked *Doom* deathmatches on their SG work stations, and they got a taste of the N64's multiplayer capabilities when they played an early, unfinished version of *Mario Kart 64*, which "provided totally incontrovertible proof that it was possible to make multiplayer, and have it be more fun," Hollis said in 2018.

But their favorite game of all was *Super Bomberman* (1993) on the SNES. The Rare office had an early prototype SNES (the British pronounce this word "snezz") console with its circuitry exposed, and the Bond team regularly gathered around it at lunchtime for vicious sessions of *Bomberman*. "Time just flew past… it got really serious, with league tables and controllers being thrown round in temper tantrums," Doak said in 2004, and even a cartridge getting angrily chucked out of a window at one point, he told me.

"I think you're going to be the one getting up and making the next pot of tea," one player might taunt another—the epitome of British smack talk.

"You're going home in a fucking ambulance," his opponent might reply, speaking a more American smack talk.

Doak has noted that *Super Bomberman* "embodies the direct multiplayer nature of console gaming… there's killing someone, and there's *telling* them you're going to kill them and *then* killing them." The Bond team found *Bomberman*'s mines completely hilarious, and they also loved the game's split-screen setup, which made "watching other people as important as watching yourself," according to Doak. These joys all made it into *GoldenEye*'s multiplayer, but it was a hard battle to make that happen.

"The will was always there to make *GoldenEye* have multiplayer," Doak said in 2019, and Hollis's early game design document does briefly mention a "Multiplayer Option" for two players with linked consoles. But at this early stage, multiplayer was a total shot in the dark—nothing more than a tentative idea on a fantasy wish list. Hollis couldn't articulate the concept more firmly at this point because he had no idea at the beginning of development that the N64 would have four controller ports.

But *GoldenEye*'s constant delays and missed deadlines meant that management frowned on adding anything extra in—meaning that multiplayer *GoldenEye* was off the table. "Once the main game was done, Nintendo told Tim and Chris Stamper that on no account were we allowed to do a multiplayer mode because that would be the height of lunacy so late in the project," Botwood explained in 2008. "So we did one." In March or April of 1997, when *GoldenEye* was already very late, and against the explicit instruction of his bosses and his bosses' bosses, Hollis decided to ask one of his team members to try and program a four-player split-screen multiplayer deathmatch mode. He gave the task to a man named Steve Ellis.

Ellis was the final addition to the *GoldenEye* team, hired just out of college six months after Doak. Ellis, who Doak calls "a phenomenal programmer," first started programming at age eight, after his parents gave him a ZX Spectrum for Christmas one year. Before he was nine, Ellis was attending college programming courses in the evening and constantly writing code for the Spectrum and Amiga, driven by the simple question, "What can I get [this machine] to do within the limits that it has?" The same question drove Ellis's work on *GoldenEye*. "Some of the things that I find personally interesting about making the game were the clever technical things," Ellis told me. "No one's looking at that kind of thing. It's just about what the experience of playing the game is. [But] part of the reason we were able to deliver that experience is because of these underlying technical things that were done to allow us to get more out of the hardware."

Ellis worked on low-level programming and optimization in *GoldenEye*, including texture mapping as well as visual effects like explosions, smoke, and bullet holes. But he also worked on many invisible projects that kept the game running, such as texture compression, microcode (with Hollis), and an original demand paging system of virtual memory that creatively maximized the N64's memory capabilities to allow more memory for textures. "Back then it was about these low-level, hardware-level hacks that you had to do to get the most out of what you've got in terms of system," Ellis told me. "I always enjoyed that stuff so that was great for me." Ellis also coded into the game a hidden, fully functional ZX Spectrum emulator along with ten games. The emulator was a side project meant to figure out if the N64 could support such an emulation.

In the end, Ellis said, Tim Stamper didn't want to include it in the release version because Rare didn't want to give the rights to the Spectrum games to Nintendo. "I disabled it, but apparently not very thoroughly," Ellis tweeted. Although the emulator isn't accessible from within the game itself, the functional code remains in the ROM. Rare did eventually make the ZX Spectrum emulator playable in *Donkey Kong 64*, where you can play the Spectrum title *Jetpac*. In the *GoldenEye* code, it exists as a kind of homage to Rare's past.

•

Ellis and Botwood, working together, took only six weeks to make *GoldenEye*'s multiplayer mode—a blistering pace by any standards. "[Ellis] coded [multiplayer] in a month, which was the work of a magician," Botwood explained later, "while I set up the spawning, weapon and ammo points and cut the level backgrounds down to a quarter of their polycount, then made new backgrounds when we didn't have enough variety. [Hilton] contributed some fantastically complex environments as well. Which meant I had to go back and do better texturing on the ones I'd made."

To create multiplayer, Ellis explained that he had "to introduce the concept of a 'player' into the game and gather all of the player's properties—their position, direction, health, ammo, animations and hundreds of others—into one place and then go through all the tens of thousands of lines of code and make sure that anything that accessed player data was aware that there might be more than one player in the game." This tedious, iterative process meant finding and fixing hundreds if not thousands of assumptions in the game code one at a time.

Coding multiplayer represented "an enormous challenge" for Ellis, according to Hollis. "Nothing was planned for displaying so many characters on the screen," he said in 2016. "The initial result was a little slow so we created smaller levels to decrease the number of polygons and optimized the code. Then, Edmonds, animation specialist, took over and polished it all. Remarkable work."

When Ellis started work on *GoldenEye*'s multiplayer, he genuinely didn't know whether it would work at all. His biggest technical hurdle was the frame rate. "[Multiplayer] was a big challenge," Hollis said later. "In the four-player game, you can see up to twelve characters on the screen, because in each of the four windows, you could see three other characters. So it's very taxing on the machine to do all that. It's not something we really envisaged, or budgeted for, from the beginning." Botwood and Hilton worked hard cutting environments down to as few polygons as possible. They pared out detail by removing individual polygons from railings on stairs and making the ceiling totally black—any optimization they could find, they tried.

Once Ellis got a playable demo working, the team quickly saw its potential and began to further refine it, just as they had with the single-player campaign. They played multiplayer mode together every night and took notes on what felt fun and what didn't. "Having worked on a few games," Edmonds told me, "I can say that it's pretty rare that you can actually play a game that you've worked on and actually enjoy it," since you get so tired of working on it and seeing the same things every day. "But I remember playing multiplayer and it was really good fun."

Botwood still remembers challenging Doak in the Archives on pistols only, no aim assist, one shot kills—"a proper duel environment," he told me. "Dave won, obviously."

The team didn't necessarily have a clear plan in mind as they playtested, but their method never led them astray. "We played [multiplayer] continually," Doak said later. "That's another reason that it's good, is that we played it. You can't make a good game that you don't enjoy." Doak added that once *GoldenEye* multiplayer became available to the other teams at Rare, they would play it in the evenings and provide additional testing and feedback, most of which was overwhelmingly positive.

The team tried out all of *GoldenEye*'s single-player levels as multiplayer levels, but spaces like Dam and Surface were too large and ran too slow. Statue and Cradle made it far enough through the design process as multiplayer levels that they can still be accessed with a GameShark, but they didn't make the final cut because Cradle had lag issues with more than two players and Statue had frame rate problems and glitch areas. And so, to keep the game's frame rate up, Hilton and Botwood designed bespoke multiplayer-only levels like Stack, Library, Complex, and Basement almost entirely around hardware performance.

The first custom multiplayer level Hilton created was Complex, a giant metal room in which he tried to mix and link together differently shaped spaces, including catwalks, balconies, and hidden secret cubby holes that make for great ambush points. "Those little cubbies [were] basically me just cheating because [Doak] and [Edmonds] were much better at multiplayer than I was," Hilton told me, admitting that he took full advantage of his insider knowledge of the levels to pop out and shoot them during testing. "It took them a couple of hours to work out what I was doing," he laughed.

The inspiration for trap points like this one was, of course, *Super Bomberman.* "It taught us a phenomenal amount about what makes competitive gameplay fun," Hilton told me. "We used all of those things that annoyed us, things that made us laugh. All of that was thrown into the multiplayer of *GoldenEye.*" And, of course, there was "Slappers Only" mode, one of the funniest things in the entire game (especially on License to Kill mode).

"The karate chop was supposed to be a slightly more lethal-looking martial arts style 'chop,'" Hilton said in 2018. "In the end, we all found the slightly 'slappy' nature of it funny—it definitely appealed to the slightly immature sense of humor that the whole team shared ["slapper" is a British slang term for a promiscuous woman]. So we kept it like it was and implemented 'Slappers Only' mode."

•

GoldenEye's multiplayer character options made the game even more fun. You could play as one of the film's major heroes or villains, of course, like Bond, Trevelyan, Xenia, and Natalya, but you could also choose one of the many soldier builds, like an Arctic Commando or a Russian Commandant—options that always felt more exciting to me. It felt like getting to play *Mario Kart* as a random Goomba—it tapped into a bigger and more exciting in-game universe. And then there were the major characters from other Bond movies, like May Day (stylized in the game as "Mayday"), Jaws, and Baron Samedi. The unusually broad license Rare got for *GoldenEye* allowed them to use anything from the Bond universe, so Jones could model any character he wanted from the entire history of Bond, a feat no game has repeated since.

Jones told me he made May Day, Jaws, and Baron Samedi because he thought they were some of the coolest characters in the Bond franchise. "May Day is a great character—she's a wonderful villain, she looked amazing, and I had a reference for her," Jones told me. "I was looking for interesting villain characters" and especially female villains, he added. Jones pointed out that while Samedi originally had a huge cross on his chest, Nintendo told him to take that out because they preferred to keep their games free of religious iconography. Most of Jones's references for *GoldenEye*'s additional characters came from his own personal collection of Bond stuff. "I had this vast array of James Bond paraphernalia," Jones said. "Before the internet existed, I was supplying all those references."

One of the funniest additional characters Jones worked into multiplayer mode was Oddjob, whose extremely short stature gives him an unfair advantage in death matches since he is a smaller target to hit. Today, Oddjob is a cultural touchstone for an entire generation of gamers: a destroyer of friendships and character choice of only the most despicable cheaters. Jones built Oddjob "because I thought he was cool and I had a picture reference for him," he told me, with little concern over how his short stature might give him an unfair advantage in a multiplayer arena. The team threw in multiplayer mode so last-minute that they didn't have enough time to balance all the characters or work out all of their kinks and idiosyncrasies. If they had had time, Hollis has noted, Oddjob might not exist in multiplayer at all. But Oddjob isn't actually short. Harold Sakata, who played Oddjob, is 5′10″, the same height as Boris's actor, Alan Cumming. As Doak speculated at a Norwich Games Festival talk, perhaps the team made Oddjob so short because they confused him with Nik Nak, the 3'11" henchman from *The Man with the Golden Gun* (1974). On the other hand, Doak noted to me, the impression that Oddjob is so short may have come from the fact that he's most famous in the movie *Goldfinger* for crouching and throwing his hat, which makes him appear shorter.

Since his inception, Oddjob has remained a very controversial character and, over the years, one of the game's most lasting inside jokes. "We all thought it was kind of cheating when we were playtesting with Oddjob," Hilton said in a group interview with MEL Magazine, "but it was too much fun to take out and there was no impetus from any of us to change it. It's clearly become part of the culture and folklore of the game."

Edmonds chimed in: "It's definitely cheating to play as Oddjob! But that can just add to the fun when you're all sitting there next to each other and berating/poking/hitting the person who chooses him. Personally I like to pick Jaws [a harder character to win with, given his enormous height and thus larger target size] and then beat the person with Oddjob just to show them! We could have put something in to stop this blatant cheating, but why not just let players decide on their own rules?"

Hollis went so far as to include Oddjob on his list of "Mistakes I Like" about *GoldenEye* at his GDC Postmortem presentation. "You can certainly make an argument that he never should have been in the game, that it would be a better game without him," he said, but your friend choosing Oddjob is a "social dynamics problem." "You should be putting pressure on your friend to not be a cheater," Hollis argued later. "People have redefined this as, 'Oddjob is what the cheater picks,' and I think that's a beautiful solution to what could be said was underbalancing. We didn't have time to balance all the characters. Really we just threw them all in for the multiplayer. But these little quirks and bits of sketchiness, I really strongly feel bring personality into the game."

This was true of all the bonus characters. Including a variety of characters from the many different eras of Bond makes the game feel true not just to a single film but to the entire Bond canon and concept. It feels like a giant fan mashup chock-full of Bond Easter eggs and homages: the laser from *Moonraker*, the electromagnetic watch from *Live and Let Die*, Jaws from *The Spy Who Loved Me*, Oddjob from *Goldfinger*, and the golden gun from *The Man with the Golden Gun*. In addition, the different controller configurations each share the name of a Bond girl—the default setting, Honey, refers to Honey Ryder from *Dr. No,* while others included Kissy Suzuki, Mary Goodnight, Domino Vitali, and Solitaire. Even the names of multiplayer game modes referenced other films: *You Only Live Twice, License to Kill,* and *The Man with the Golden Gun.*

One of the coolest Bond universe references sadly didn't make it into the final version of the game. *GoldenEye's* multiplayer originally included three other James Bonds besides Pierce Brosnan: Sean Connery, Roger Moore, and Timothy

Dalton. "So you could have four friends [playing as] the four different Bonds, which was awesome," Hollis explained in 2018. "Because everyone has an opinion about who the best Bond is. And it's a very matey moment." Jones mapped all four of the actors' faces onto his Bond models, each of which he outfitted with a different tuxedo: Connery wore a white tux with a rose corsage, Dalton an open tux, and Moore a double-breasted tux. The four Bonds would have been available not only in multiplayer but in single-player, as well—and as a game setting option rather than a cheat.

"On the folder screen where you choose between the four saved games you could switch between the different Bonds for a new saved game by using the D-pad," Edmonds said later.

"We liked the idea of playing through the game a second or third time as Roger Moore or Sean Connery," Doak said. "You wouldn't see it apart from the cutscenes."

But alas, near the end of development, MGM studio executives paid the barn a visit one day and put an end to the three other Bonds. Doak, who was in the middle of setting up the Aztec level, showed them the level's starring villain, Baron Samedi, "and they were quite pleased we had Samedi in it because he was an iconic character," Doak said in 2018. "So we showed them we had all the Bonds... Well, soon after that we got a memo saying we couldn't have all the Bonds, because only the *GoldenEye* actors had signed off on the digital rights to their likeness to be used in games, not the older movies." Apparently including all four Bonds would have required working out deals with each Bond actor's agent and would have cost as much as one million dollars for just one of the actors.

To send the other three Bonds off with style, the team played an epic three-hour long deathmatch—first to a hundred kills—on the day they had to take them out. At the very last moment, Edmonds, playing as Moore, won by one kill. While Moore won the deathmatch, Connery's Bond survived in early promotional footage of the game, and even in the instruction manual. You can still find all four Bonds in the game's ROM and play as them in certain mods—and the dinner jackets are all available in *Perfect Dark*'s Combat Simulator.

•

Ken Lobb took so many trips to Twycross to visit Rare as a Nintendo rep that they'd come to have a usual routine and rhythm to them. But this trip was different. No sooner had he entered the Bond barn when Martin Hollis dragged him into a conference room and plunked him into a chair in front of an N64 with a prototype *GoldenEye* cartridge and four controllers. They fired up *GoldenEye* and played fifteen minutes of multiplayer—and Lobb was blown away

"This is incredible," he stammered out to Hollis. "It's awesome."

"We want to delay the game six months to add this in," Hollis answered.

"You want to what?" Lobb responded, dumbstruck. "We're already eight months late!"

Lobb's play session was the first Nintendo management had ever heard about multiplayer's existence, but "since the game was already late by that time, if we hadn't done it that way, it probably never would have happened," Hollis noted in 2012.

The play session made a huge impact on Lobb. "It's one of those moments in time that's literally photographically burned into my memory," Lobb said recently. The multiplayer mode was just that good.

And so Lobb acquiesced. "This is too fun," he said to Hollis in the conference room. "Let me add it." Ellis told me that Lobb asked him to hide the multiplayer mode but keep it accessible via a controller button combination so that he could dramatically reveal it to the Nintendo of America Treehouse staff in-person. Somehow, Lobb managed to convince Howard Lincoln to let the team have the additional time they needed to finish multiplayer development.

The extra time allowed the team to add in a revolutionary number of different game modes and customizable settings, which made gameplay all the more addicting and endlessly novel. Playing License to Kill with sniper rifles in Caverns, for instance, offers an entirely different experience than playing Living Daylights (a.k.a. Capture the Flag) with remote mines in Facility. The team included such a diverse array of gameplay options, Botwood told me, to make multiplayer as adaptable as possible. "There was always a new mode to try or a new option to play with if you wanted something different," he explained in a later interview. And because everyone could specialize in certain levels and certain weapons settings, everyone had a chance at winning, which meant more competitive, exciting gameplay.

GoldenEye's multiplayer design suited it perfectly for the party or couch hangout setting. The simple controls and auto-aim meant a smaller learning curve for new casual players to jump in, and multiplayer mode was fun to watch if you had to sit out for a round. The split-screen style, which some today consider one of the game's drawbacks, ended up being one of its greatest strengths. "Everyone was saying at that time that [multiplayer] wouldn't be any fun with split-screen, [that] it wouldn't be any good," Hollis said just after the game's release. "And I was kind of listening to those remarks and believing them, but they turned out to be completely false because if you're sitting beside the other three people, you can shout and scream at them—you can see their reactions in a way that you can't when it's on a network."

Many of us who grew up with *GoldenEye* feel nostalgic for just this feeling—of sitting on a couch with three or more friends, clustered around a tiny TV screen, sharing a bag of Doritos, laughing while you blew each other up with remote mines. "To this day," Doak affirmed in 2019, "I think […] one of the highlights of video gaming is people sitting in the same space enjoying the social banter and ribbing and tough love that happens when you're playing couch multiplayer, whether it's a co-op or a competitive game or whatever—it's a really marvelous thing." For Millennial gamers, *GoldenEye*'s goofy, lighthearted spirit and couch-based multiplayer reflect the last few years of our collective innocence. We shot each other lovingly and hilariously, without a care in the world. And we were together the whole time we did it.

Many nostalgic fans lament the loss of this intimate, connected experience. *GoldenEye*'s multiplayer, journalist Simon Parkin told me, represents a way of playing video games that has increasingly been replaced by online multiplayer. "When you're playing a well-designed video game with your friends, it's as much about the conversation—the being together, eating pizza, and making jokes as it is about winning," Parkin told me.

Hollis himself considers the "solitaryisation" and "atomisation" of online gaming a great shame. "It is more convenient for people, but it is less emotive," he said in 2010. "The best experiences I've ever had playing games has been with one, two, or three other friends, all in a room, playing anything from *Super Bomberman* onwards. I think it's a shame that there are so many games that support this one person on their own, this alone style of playing with other people, and not so many that support more togetherness."

Norgate puts it more simply: "It's quite a different experience playing in the same room and being able to elbow the person next to you because they've shot you in the face."

Local multiplayer isn't just more fun—it also keeps us more civil. Anytime I played *GoldenEye* with friends, we certainly teased each other, but our insults and taunts were never vicious. We even had our own unspoken code of sportsmanship—unwritten rules, just as the team had intended us to make on our own, like "No Oddjob," "No Camping Near Respawn Locations," and my personal favorite, the Mercy Rule—you don't kill someone if they haven't had time to pick up a gun yet.

But contemporary online multiplayer games are inhabited by griefers, flamers, teabaggers, and bullies regularly hurling out death or rape threats and racist or misogynistic slurs. The phenomenon is so common that a recent survey revealed that one out of every two gamers had experienced online bullying or harassment, and 47 percent had been threatened. Another study put that number closer to 78 percent, and that study was focused on *Animal Crossing*, a very innocuous game about living in a village with goofy cartoon animals. The etiquette around online gaming has matched the etiquette of the internet at large. We tend to treat our video game foes better when we know them and can see them sitting right there in front of us—when we're not anonymous and have to maintain a relationship with our combatant beyond the death match arena, as roommates or soccer teammates or cousins.

And so, at the surprisingly early age of 33, I've already become the crotchety old-timer yelling, "Back in my day, we gamers were all nicer to each other!" Today, *GoldenEye*'s implicit code of conduct feels as charming as it does antiquated, like your grandfather carrying around a handkerchief with his initials stitched into it. And the memories of being with your friends in your basement staying up all night playing *GoldenEye* and drinking Mountain Dew—those memories matter a great deal, and it's not just because we all grew up.

In the end, as enjoyable as the single-player campaigns were, *GoldenEye*'s local competitive multiplayer made it the hit title it was, leaving an enormous impact on the gaming industry as a whole by proving that party-based multiplayer games could be successful at a time when console-based contemporaries like *Turok* and *Doom 64* (1997) offered no multiplayer. *GoldenEye* was "the first truly popular multiplayer console shooter," and present-day console shooters continue striving to meet the standards for fun that *GoldenEye* set 25 years ago.

Beyond the sales success, critical praise, or even lasting impact on the industry, the development team is proud to have worked on a multiplayer mode that meant so much to so many friendships. "I've been blamed many times, over the years, for failed degrees or underachieving exam results caused by too many late-night *GoldenEye* deathmatch sessions," Hilton told MEL Magazine. "It's great to know you've made a lasting impression on people's lives!"

KILLER APP

THE JUNE 1997 E3 CONFERENCE met for three days in sweltering Atlanta, Georgia, inside the massive Georgia Dome. 500 exhibitors debuted 1,500 new titles, advertising with leather-clad booth babes, life-size Arwings and Mario karts, and at least one professional model impersonating Lara Croft. Although *Resident Evil 2, Final Fantasy VII*, and *Metal Gear Solid* all debuted here, PC first-person shooters mainly stole the show, with a ton of excitement around games like *Half-Life, Doom* creator John Romero's new title *Daikatana*, and id Software's *Quake II*.

Meanwhile, Nintendo's N64 still had a woefully sparse library of titles. Rare held such an important role with Nintendo that Rare made up the entirety of Nintendo's Christmas 1997 titles, which meant that at E3 1997, Nintendo's booth was functionally a Rare booth. Huge banners of Banjo and Conker hung from the ceiling, along with a wall of eight consoles on which conference attendees could try out an early working version of *GoldenEye*, surrounded by cardboard cutouts of Pierce Brosnan.

The *GoldenEye* screens went largely unnoticed, however, as platformer *Banjo-Kazooie* stole all the thunder. "The first couple days of the show, it was complete tumbleweed," Doak said in 2017.

When people did come up to play *GoldenEye*, Hollis remembered, the things he overheard them saying about it left him "extremely pained." While some people praised the game, others completely hated it. Meanwhile, Botwood and Doak remember Hollis getting holed up with Nintendo for days on end haggling over which of the game's remaining bugs the team had time to fix.

"It would be fair to say that critical expectations were very low," Hollis said later. They were so low that most journalists and PC gamers passed right by the *GoldenEye* stand without even stopping, assuming that the game was nothing more than another boring *Doom* clone. It's possible, too, that show attendees were confused by all the paraphernalia from *GoldenEye* the film, which had come out "an embarrassing two years ago," Hollis noted later. "We shouldn't have gone to E3," Hollis surmised. "We should have been back at Twycross fixing bugs."

GoldenEye had gone over very well amongst the other teams at Rare ("there was even an internal trade in illicit multiplayer ROMs," Doak told Nintendo Life), and Nintendo corporate had congratulated the team on their exceptionally high internal testing score. But

E3 had gone so badly, Doak said, that the team was extremely nervous.

Although more and more people began visiting the Nintendo booth to play *GoldenEye* as E3 went on, Hollis noted that he and Edmonds felt "slightly depressed" at how poorly *GoldenEye* had gone over at the convention, especially since, once they got back to Rare, they had only a few weeks left to fix around 500 bugs, with Nintendo calling every day to check in during the last few months of development.

Once they arrived back in Twycross, the team put their heads down and kept working. Lobb reassured them the game would be a hit. And to encourage his colleagues in this final sprint to the finish line, Hollis printed out the game's box art on one of Rare's few color printers and folded it up into a cartridge-sized box—a tantalizing reminder of the finished product that lay just around the corner. "I wanted to give the team an idea that this game would actually be finished soon because it had been a really long slog," Hollis said in 2013.

The team spent the summer of 1997 fixing bugs faxed to them by Nintendo. They would sit down every morning, divide up all the bugs, read them out loud, and whoever knew where to find them would volunteer to fix them. The bugs weren't exactly minor, either. In a 2017 presentation, Doak shared a list of them from the era, which included half a dozen ways that the game would freeze, black out, or crash. Devastating results could be triggered simply by entering a certain room or pressing certain button combinations; in short, the team had their work cut out from them.

One of the most infamous bugs Nintendo reported to the team, Hilton told me, was that characters in the distance grew smaller. "We rather pissily told them, 'Well, it's a 3D game—of course they get smaller—it's perspective,'" he remembered. "And then someone checked it and discovered that they were actually right—there was a scaling issue that made characters scale down as they went farther away. So they spotted that and we hadn't. They were very good, Nintendo in Japan—they spotted everything and we got very little past them."

Amid all this bug-fixing, Jones made promotional art renders and worked with Edmonds to "hastily put together" a design for the front-end loading screen, where players choose game modes and save files. "We were going to have an opening sequence with the [Bond] girls coming out of the barrels and dancing but we crammed so much in by that point that we had just run out of memory," Jones told me.

At first, Edmonds wanted players to have to select a dossier from the menu screen using a crosshair controlled by the analog stick—a subtle way to teach them the game's controls. But then Rare production manager Simon Farmer offered him some important advice. "I'd never had a Nintendo console when I was growing up," Edmonds told me, "[but] one of the key things with Nintendo games is that when the game starts up, all you ever have to do to get into the game is just press the

A button, and that's it. My initial menu system wasn't like that at all [...] One of the things that came out of speaking to Simon was to always make sure that that crosshair on the front end is over the default option, so then you just press A and then it just takes you straight through into the game." Anyone who has fired up their N64 and hurriedly pressed A A A A A A to get into a saved game of *GoldenEye* has witnessed firsthand the results of this change. And if you've noticed the "On Her Majesty's Secret Service" logo on the file folders, you have Hilton to thank—he scanned the logo in from his passport.

Meanwhile, Ellis programmed in cheats after a quick discussion in the office about how funny it would be to give all the characters huge heads. "I'm not sure who thought of all the different types of cheats, but it probably includes ideas from everyone on the team," Edmonds said in 2018. "I think different programmers added in different cheats: I added the Big Head mode [known in-game as DK Mode] as I wrote all the animation software, and it's probably my favorite as it looks so ridiculous." Other cheats included unlocking secret levels and more multiplayer characters, invisibility, invincibility, max ammo, paintball mode, and "all guns" mode. "There were certainly a lot more cheats available during development which got removed," Edmonds said in another interview, including maximum ammo, super health and armor, and a line mode that makes everything look like it's been sketched with a pencil.

(Although it was never fun enough to include, it did prove helpful for debugging purposes.)

GoldenEye was one of the first games to feature unlockable rewards, and while many games today offer cheats as paid downloadable content, *GoldenEye*'s players had to earn them all through good old-fashioned hard work—specifically, by time trial. While the rest of the team wanted to hold back the codes and release them in magazines, Lobb said later, "I'd been fixated my whole career on 'gameplay unlocks cool things, and if you're [good], you should be able to unlock really cool things. So I wrote a big spec about how I wanted to have special unlocks in every level and I pitched [it] to them." He then used Nintendo's testing department to determine the times required to unlock a cheat—for instance, beating the Runway level on Agent mode in less than five minutes unlocks Big Head mode.

This approach to cheats neatly linked *GoldenEye*'s multiplayer mode with its single-player campaign, journalist Simon Parkin told me: "You would want to collectively try and achieve these [times] in the single-player to unlock new humor or gameplay in the multiplayer," he said.

The team left button code cheats in the game partly "as a safety measure," Edmonds said later, "so that if the game turned out to be too hard or we wanted to make sure everyone could access a particular cheat or level then we could just release the code in the future."

Button codes also acted as debug tools for the developers and Nintendo's testers, Botwood said in the same interview. "We believed quite strongly in not having these shortcuts," he added. "We thought that the special modes and other levels should be earned by the player rather than gifted to them, so we didn't want to include the button codes for *GoldenEye 007*; including the codes in the final game was not the team's decision. However, since we had to include them, we made them obtuse and difficult so you wouldn't find them by accident."

Another eleventh-hour addition to the game was a set of unlockable bonus levels called Aztec and Egyptian. Hollis had originally envisioned eighteen levels for the single-player campaign, but the team wanted to add two more to fill out the 4x5 grid on the menu-select screen with a nice, neat number. "We wanted some bonus levels as a reward for the player, and the license we had allowed us to make use of anything from previous Bond films," Edmonds said later. "Those particular elements were picked because they are real classics and were favourites of people on the team."

"In retrospect, twenty levels was insane," Doak said in 2008, but he noted elsewhere that "When we made those games, we tried to put everything that we would want as a consumer into the game, so everything that's now DLC were in the game."

The two bonus levels also allowed the developers to take more advantage of their all-inclusive Bond license and "use a bit more of our knowledge of the James Bond universe," Jones explained.

Aztec, an enormous ruin hiding a space shuttle launch site, was inspired by *Moonraker* (1979), one of the Bond franchise's campiest films and one of its only dips into sci-fi. And although the addition of the film's 7′2″, steel-toothed villain Jaws into the level was cool, what really captured the imagination of 90s kids was the inclusion of the space shuttle. Hilton told me he's particularly proud of Aztec, which he made toward the end of development when he was more confident with the technology. He made the space shuttle by repurposing the textures for the satellite in the Silo level, and the shuttle's lift-off is made of repurposed grenade explosions. "It was lots of bits and pieces hammered together," Hilton told me.

"We really wanted to make sure the bonus levels really were a reward, and the artists and level designers were at the peak of their performance," an anonymous team member said later. After setting up the level, Doak and Hollis played through Aztec on 00 Agent and each beat it after a few hours.

"Being the mischievous pair that we are," Hollis noted later, "I said to [Doak], 'Ok that's good. Now why don't you just make it a little bit harder,' so Aztec is just slightly harder than we were able to do ourselves at the time, and in my opinion it's arguably the hardest level in the game on 00, but I still get a great deal of satisfaction from playing it, although it can be frustrating at times."

Egyptian, the second bonus mission, which takes place in an Egyptian temple, is kind of bonkers. First, it breaks a central pact with the gamer: that once you kill a bad guy, he's really dead (okay, at least *within the same level* he usually stays dead). Instead, you have to kill voodoo master Baron Samedi *three times* in Egyptian, since he's famous for cheating death in the movie *Live and Let Die*. But then he comes back to life yet again in the final cutscene! In addition to an outrageous boss battle, Egyptian also featured an outrageous puzzle. In order to unlock the mythical Golden Gun, which kills most enemies in only one shot, players had to walk across floor tiles in a very particular pattern or get shot with darts. This type of troll puzzle, which could only be solved through repeated trial and error or the help of a *Nintendo Power* strategy guide, is extremely uncommon in games today.

After the cheats and bonus levels were added and *GoldenEye* was tested and scoured for bugs, it went through "lot check," a two-week process of playing the game to death on various types of televisions. In these final days, testers reported back a fairly serious problem: on one of the levels, (probably Frigate), if you played it in a certain order, the characters would appear with awful-looking textures due to a glitch in the game's dynamic memory system. In a single day, Hollis had to make a few particularly clever last-minute hacks to the ROM that would get it working with as minimal a touch as possible to the game's code. With that final eleventh-hour adjustment made, and without recompiling anything, Hollis sent the ROM back to Nintendo. *GoldenEye* was finally finished.

•

"What did you do after *GoldenEye*?" I asked Edmonds during our interview. His answer? "Slept." After the massive crunch of the final few weeks, the team needed to rest and recover. And so, he explained, they shared a meal at a local restaurant and then started waiting for the reviews to come in, finally enjoying the relief of time to breathe.

Finishing the game, Hollis said later, felt a little anticlimactic, "but there was a certain amount of pleasure being able to look at things that nearly three years before had just been a few words." Edmonds recently remembered Tim Stamper asking the team what they would rate the game, and Edmonds told him 7 out of 10.

"We all felt it could have been better," Hilton said, and while they all felt relieved to be finished, Doak said, they were also "incredibly self-critical."

"All we could see were the bad things," Doak added: "the compromises and cuts which had been necessary to get the thing finished."

GoldenEye was released in Japan on August 23, 1997 and two days later in the US and Europe. It retailed for $69.95—$112.49 in 2021's inflation-adjusted dollars—to a gaming community that believed three core truths: licensed games sucked, only PC gamers played first-person shooters, and Rare specialized in platformers. *GoldenEye* was about to blow all of these "truths" out of the water.

On August 19, Nintendo hosted a launch party for the game at Club Chaos in New York City. Grace Jones (the actress who played May Day in *A View to a Kill*) and Maud Adams (the actress who played Octopussy in 1983's *Octopussy*) came to the party and even played the game. "I've tried the game," Adams said in an interview at the event, "and I really got caught up in the suspense and the intrigue, and I really felt as though I was part of this world—I felt like I was making the movie again." TV ads from the era took this same strategy, intercutting clips from *GoldenEye* the film with clips from *GoldenEye* the game to emphasize that you are James Bond in a game based on the movie. To the tune of the Bond theme song, text on the screen reads, "Introducing *GoldenEye 007*… The first Bond adventure where you direct the action—shot by shot." Get it?

GoldenEye's sales accumulated slowly, and initially they looked somewhat disappointing. "It wasn't apparent that *GoldenEye* was going to be as successful as it was until four, five months after it came out," Doak told Nintendo Life in 2020. "It reviewed very well, but the sales were quite slow at the start" due to the lag time required for cartridge manufacture and distribution. *GoldenEye* sold at a slow burn for the first few months, and Rare didn't know how successful the game really was until they saw the data on rentals in the US.

Lobb had made a controversial move at Nintendo of America by taking a big risk on rentals. He sent a copy of *GoldenEye* to every Blockbuster in the country, with the assurance that if they didn't want it anymore after 60 days, they could send it back. "No one sent them back," Lobb said years later. "We became the number-one rented game at Blockbuster for like three years." According to the Video Software Dealers Association's rental charts, *GoldenEye* stayed on the top rental charts for *75 weeks* and topped the list at number one all the way into March 1998.

Thanks to a slow burn of word-of-mouth publicity, *GoldenEye*'s sales steadily increased and hit their first big spike around Christmas 1997, when cartridges were so coveted that the retail price spiked to more than $100. "It's just not on the shelves anywhere," said a California electronics store owner at the time. "Some people are really gouging their customers who want it now." "Demand was so great," a journalist wrote in 1997, "that Toys 'R' Us offered to fly 75,000 units of *GoldenEye 007* from Japan into the United States to ensure they had it on the shelves for Christmas."

The team watched in horror as gamers in online forums complained that *GoldenEye* was sold out everywhere around the holiday season. "[It] was really frustrating for the team," Ellis said later.

"Initially, I think Nintendo only made around 1 to 2 million cartridges, and we kept hearing stories of how people were searching for the game in shops that had sold out," Hilton said in 2018. He explained to me that "in those days, a game had quite a short shelf life—it was on the shelf for a few months and then it was in the bargain bucket quite quickly after that, so we assumed Christmas was our big chance and if we missed Christmas, then that would be it." "But we were lucky that people still wanted it and it kept selling," he added.

After Nintendo restocked the shelves with cartridges, sales took off again, especially in mid-1998 when the N64's price dropped from $149 to $129. All in all, gaming hardware and software sales increased by almost 20% from 1997 to 1998, with software sales in particular jumping by 58%. By the end of 1998, *GoldenEye* had sold 2.1 million copies. making it the rare title that sold more in its second year than its first year. "When [word of] the multiplayer started to kick in, it was like a rocket," Kirkhope told me.

"In my opinion, the game benefited from the license for the first few months; then the success was all about word of mouth," Lobb said in 2020.

Sales climbed yet again in 1999, when Nintendo included the game as part of its "Player's Choice" series of discounted hits. An entertainment store manager noted at the time that the reduced price made *GoldenEye* rebound in sales and return to the top ten list, and an analysis from the era confirmed that games in the

Player's Choice program sold better than any others. In the end, *GoldenEye* sold more copies in the UK in 1999 than 1997 and 1998 combined.

In the few years after its release, *GoldenEye* sold more than eight million copies and made $250 million total globally—nearly double the amount the movie had grossed worldwide. *GoldenEye* ended up the third best-selling N64 game of all time, after *Mario Kart 64* and *Super Mario 64,* making it the best-selling N64 game not made in-house by Nintendo. And although sales like *GoldenEye*'s are not uncommon for today's big games, at the time, these numbers signaled very impressive global market penetration.

The game's success came as a shock to the team. "Anyone in the industry with a bit of wisdom will tell you [that] it's always very unclear whether a game's going to be a success or not," Hollis told Game Developer. "No one ever came to me and said, 'You know that game you made, that's going to sell eight million units.' No one could have predicted it. Nintendo couldn't have predicted it, and it has people whose job it is to predict sales."

During all this time, Botwood and Doak would print reviews off the one computer at Rare connected to the internet and pin them up on the team bulletin board. "I particularly remember reading IGN's very positive review by Doug Perry," Doak said in a [year] interview. "Later, the UK print review in *Edge* was another big sigh of relief, and something that mattered a lot to us on the team because it was so respected."

In that review, the author called *GoldenEye* a "truly masterful first-person gem" and "the best single-player first-person game on any system." He awarded the game 10/10 for presentation, gameplay, and lasting appeal, and 9/10 for graphics and sound. He noted that the game "feels, looks and sounds exactly like the movie" and praised "unique level objectives, tight control, unsurpassed weapons and multiplayer mode," which "unleash[ed] the full power of Nintendo's four-player capabilities."

Journalist after journalist showered *GoldenEye* with praise. "It's very difficult for me to describe a game that is so close to perfection," one reviewer wrote, while another called it "an intelligently conceived and brilliantly executed diamond of a game." "If you only have enough money for one game every six months, *GoldenEye 007* is the one to get," noted *N64 Gazetta*, which named *GoldenEye* Best Game, Best Graphics, and Best Multiplayer of the Year 1997. Many pointed out that it was the game N64 players had been waiting for since finishing *Super Mario 64* or simply that it was the best N64 game they had ever played. One reviewer, thinking ahead, called it a "pure classic" while another, left seemingly speechless, wrote simply, "In a word: Wow. We're still trying to catch our breath after playing this one; it's that good."

Many critics discussed how the game let you feel just like Bond, thanks to the gadgets, weapons, and mission objectives that "force you to think like smarty-pants

Bond himself." The game's stealth mechanics and artificial intelligence received tons of praise. Electric Playground, awarding the game a score of 9.5 out of 10, noted that "Where *GoldenEye* sets itself apart from the rest of the first-person shooter pack, is the fact that a quick trigger finger and uncanny aim will not win the game for you…" Another reviewer went so far as to argue that *GoldenEye*'s stealth gameplay evolved the entire FPS genre by asking players to think like spies and operate strategically. Game Center made an equally bold claim, arguing that the multiplayer mode "exceed[ed] any PC or console multiplayer game on the market."

GoldenEye won a slew of awards in the few years after its release, including the very prestigious BAFTA Interactive Entertainment Games Award and four more from the Academy of Interactive Arts & Sciences, who honored *GoldenEye* with an Outstanding Achievement in Software Engineering award. The fierce competition that year included *Final Fantasy VII, Quake II, Resident Evil 2, Turok: Dinosaur Hunter*, and *Riven*, the sequel to 1993's *Myst*. The *GoldenEye* team called Rare with the good news at 2 a.m. the night of the awards ceremony, after returning to their hotel from a well-deserved night of celebrating. The game also swept the 1997 *Nintendo Power* awards, determined by popular vote amongst readers (only Nintendo games competed, of course, since Nintendo itself published *Nintendo Power* magazine). *GoldenEye* won thirteen awards, including Coolest

Ride (for the tank), Best Party Game Since Twister, and the Golden Bandage award (for the headshot feature).

In fact, *GoldenEye* won or placed second for every single *Nintendo Power* award except two it didn't qualify for (best sports game and best racing game) and one it probably didn't want to win—the "More-Annoying-than the-Spice Girls" award ("Fox, get this guy off me" from *Star Fox 64* won and "ow ow ow ow ow" from *Mario Kart 64* came in second). While one might dismiss all these awards as a mere Nintendo publicity stunt, they do indicate the intense fan loyalty around *GoldenEye*, which beat out very popular games like *Turok*, *Diddy Kong Racing*, and even Nintendo in-house titles like *Star Fox 64* and *Mario Kart 64* for each prize.

Perhaps the biggest lesson from all this acclaim is that no one could predict how this game would resonate with fans. Not Rare's higher-ups, not E3 attendees, not even the developers themselves. Maybe all great games feel like they arrive entirely out of the blue, hitting it big seemingly as randomly as majorly hyped titles flop. *GoldenEye*'s sequels make this clearer than ever.

NEVER SAY NEVER AGAIN

GIVEN ALL ITS WILD SUCCESS, it seems surprising that *GoldenEye* never became a franchise or series. Why isn't there a new *GoldenEye* game every few years like *Call of Duty*, *Halo*, and *Gears of War*? In the aftermath of the original, every attempt at a sequel or even just another decent James Bond game has failed to recapture lighting in a bottle. *GoldenEye* became the measuring stick against which all other James Bond games have been compared, and none of them have ever come close.

Nintendo did offer Rare the opportunity to make a game based on *Tomorrow Never Dies*, and the *GoldenEye* team even visited the film set, but ultimately they declined. "We were pretty much Bonded-out," Doak told Nintendo Life. "There's only so much Soviet-era stuff you can endure. And at the time we were competing with things like *Turok*, and they all had carte blanche to do whatever they wanted with baddies and weapons and so on. If we made another Bond game, it'd be like the second album and people wouldn't think we've really innovated."

"*GoldenEye* was three years long," Hollis said in 2020. "You know, it was a very intense development, and we spent a lot of time in the Bond universe. And really, we just had enough of that, and we wanted to stretch our legs and try out some fresh ideas."

And so, after *James Bond 007* for the Gameboy in 1998 and a *GoldenEye 007* racing game for the Virtual Boy cancelled during development, Nintendo never made another Bond game again. Rabid *GoldenEye* fans hungry for a sequel pounded on Rare's doors for an answer. In Rare's archived web forums, one commenter in 2000 complains about the lack of a *GoldenEye* PC port while another, writing in September 1999, whines: "Why did you never release any mission packs or new levels/weapons for *GoldenEye*? […] Do you not realise the demand for more levels and weapons for the game???? […] I seriously think you guys must be underestimating the demand for more *GoldenEye* stuff as the lack of any sort of level/weapon update makes no commercial sense."

But no matter how much fans complained, and despite the fortune in sales that *GoldenEye* had amassed, both Nintendo and Rare upper management respected the *GoldenEye* team members' decision to work on something entirely different—possibly because the cost of the Bond license had skyrocketed by this point. The result was an FPS sequel to *GoldenEye* that wasn't actually a sequel at all, but more of a spiritual successor: *Perfect Dark*.

Made by a development team three times larger than the *GoldenEye* team, and including almost all of the original *GoldenEye* team members, *Perfect Dark* ran on the *GoldenEye* engine and therefore shared its gameplay feel, but managed to cram in way more features and push the limits of the N64 even farther. The team could integrate wilder ideas originally pitched as jokes—like a laptop gun, an alien conspiracy, and the ability to see through walls—into a sci-fi universe more easily than the Bond universe, and things the team couldn't get working or couldn't fit into *GoldenEye* made it into *Perfect Dark*, too—for instance, Bond's unused motorbike became a hoverbike.

Perfect Dark starred a new character in a new story in a different genre—a techno dystopia. Rare let the team make up their own story and hero from scratch, which presented its own set of challenges. While players already knew James Bond well, *Perfect Dark*'s secret agent Joanna Dark (named after Joan of Arc) was entirely unknown.

GoldenEye's wild success meant added pressure on *Perfect Dark*. "They were constantly trying to live up to what was happening all around the world with *GoldenEye 007*, which was growing in popularity literally every month for most of the *Perfect Dark* dev cycle," Lobb told Eurogamer. "That internal pressure to live up to *GoldenEye 007* was constant."

Edmonds remembers this not as pressure, necessarily, but rather as "incentive to try and make [*Perfect*

Dark] better. It was just cool having the response to *GoldenEye*. After the two, three years we'd been working on it, it helped keep us going and encouraged us to put the hard work in again on *Perfect Dark*."

In the end, *Perfect Dark* offered better graphics, more sophisticated AI, and larger levels than *GoldenEye*, as well as voice acting, reloading animations, and more customizable options for multiplayer, including a co-op mode and AI bots to play against. After three years of development and many delays, *Perfect Dark* debuted in May 2000. Unfortunately, despite glowing reviews from the games press (*Perfect Dark* is Rare's highest-rated game on Metacritic), three years later it had only sold 1.3 million copies. The game suffered from a release date too close to the next console generation; 2000 was very late in the N64's lifecycle, and all N64 games after 2000 performed worse.

Nintendo lost its behemoth status in the games industry in the 2000s after the botched Virtual Boy and the lackluster GameCube. But Chris Kohler, in a 2007 *Wired* piece called "Nintendo's Biggest Mistakes," blames Nintendo's floundering on their decision not to make a *GoldenEye* sequel available for the GameCube at launch. "This was absolutely imperative and they didn't even realize it," Kohler writes. Kohler argues that *GoldenEye* is all that attracted older gamers to the N64, and that *Perfect Dark* should have been a launch-day GameCube title to draw in that demographic. "The game industry could have looked very different had they made that move," Kohler writes.

After Rare passed on the Bond license in 1998, it ended up with EA, who put out a disappointing Bond game every year after that like clockwork. The games included first-person shooters, third-person-shooters, and car racing games, some based on actual Bond films and others with original stories set in the Bond universe. Clearly, for these eight years, EA was just trying to throw a bunch of ideas at the wall and see what might stick. *GoldenEye* had "essentially print[ed] money for Rare and Nintendo," N64 Today founder Martin Watts told me, "and quite rightly people wanted to get in on that and try to develop the next *GoldenEye*." And so EA tried to make games very similar to *GoldenEye* and, when that didn't work, games very different from *GoldenEye*. They tried to include Pierce Brosnan and Judi Dench's voices and to capture the feel of being Bond—one game even gave you extra points when you did something that looked cool. In 2004, they put out one of the worst Bond games ever made: the misleadingly titled *GoldenEye: Rogue Agent*, which proved totally unrelated to the original and was reamed by gamers and the press.

After this catastrophic failure, EA lost the Bond license to Activision, who gave their first Bond project to Treyarch, an American developer best known for their work on the Call of Duty series. Treyarch used the *Call of Duty 4* engine to make a game based on *Quantum of Solace*, released in 2008. In the end, despite the several shout-outs to *GoldenEye*, *007: Quantum of Solace* received only mixed reviews.

2010 saw the debut of yet another spiritual successor with another confusing title: *GoldenEye 007*, which is the exact same title as the original. The game's creators at Activision Blizzard felt that a full remake of the N64 *GoldenEye 007* would be impossible because modern gamers had such different expectations, so they decided on a reimagining that combined elements from *GoldenEye* the movie, *GoldenEye* the game, modern Bond movies starring Daniel Craig, and modern games like *Call of Duty*. The game featured more explosions, movements, melee moves, and multiplayer options. Instead of a Q-issued watch, Craig's Bond used his smartphone, which contained within it most of the original game's freestanding gadgets. Other updates from the original included regenerating health (unless you play on Classic mode); reloading animations; secondary modes for weapons, like adding a silencer to a pistol; cool silent takedowns, which added to the fun of stealth; and no Boris. The game's graphics were quite good, and many levels from the original reappeared, albeit with different layouts and sometimes different names.

Unfortunately, even this painstakingly, lovingly reimagined *GoldenEye* couldn't quite stand on its own two feet. Critical reactions to the game can best be summed up by something games historian Carl Therrien told me: "no game can measure up to *GoldenEye*—not even *GoldenEye*."

Although critics reviewed the game favorably, especially the multiplayer, they couldn't help but compare the new title to the original and find it lacking. The 2010 game "carries the almost impossible weight of nostalgic expectation on [its] shoulders," one reviewer wrote, while a Vice reporter spared absolutely no punches, calling the game "the mere skin of *GoldenEye* pulled taut over lifeless, joyless, humourless design, the kind we've gotten used to over the past decade."

In the end, the reimagining's updates only reveal what made the original so special. The 2010 game's shift from "slappers only" to "melee only" "is almost the same [as the original]," one reviewer noted, "but perhaps not as hilarious at three in the morning with three other slightly inebriated chums." *GoldenEye*'s goofiness—its messiness, even—is lost in a game as slick as the 2010 *GoldenEye*. The Daniel Craig stunt double and martial arts expert who did all the 2010 game's motion-capture acting contrasted sharply with Duncan Botwood in a smelly suit getting beat up by sweet British nerds. But "bigger" isn't always better. You can feel it as you play the two: the 2010 *GoldenEye* was created by a corporation, and *GoldenEye* by human beings.

Hollis shared this vision of the remake, telling *Official Nintendo Magazine* at the time, "I imagine it is a business decision isn't it? This name is valuable, let's use it. I find it hard to picture Activision's top management being excited about the original and wanting to do it justice. In fact, I find it hard to imagine them being excited about any game." To Hollis and the rest of the team, the remake felt personal. "It's inevitable," he said in 2010. "You see it as your baby. Even when they ask, 'Do you want to be involved?' and you say no, it's still something that's connected to you and to your personality and that you want to cherish somehow. So there's maybe some irritation, or insecurity that comes out of that. That someone else is running with that ball, but then again it is pleasing that it still has currency, that the name is still valued. And how many games have been remade twice?"

"I kind of feel sorry for all the people who've worked on the [remake]," Hilton told me. "I know a few people who worked on it […] I used to tease them quite a lot about rehashing my stuff from ten years ago, but it is a bit of a poison chalice: It's like when they remake a movie and if you love the original movie, even though the new movie might have better special effects, you've already made your attachment to the original one."

Why not just rerelease the original for the Wii Virtual Console or the Xbox Live Arcade (XBLA), then? For six months in 2007, Rare was planning just that—they were working, in strict secrecy, on a remastered version for the XBLA that kept everything about the original intact but smoothed out the textures and sped up the framerate from the original 15-30 to a whip-fast 60 frames per second. The remaster added new multiplayer levels, including Frigate, Dam, and Depot. The remaster even featured an option to toggle between original graphics and updated graphics with just the tap of a bumper button. Heading up the project was none other than Mark Edmonds, who told VGC that working on the re-master "was like revisiting an old friend from the past. "The idea was to really keep the Xbox version true to the original. So it was intended for fans of the first game and to improve it in ways we could, while still staying faithful to that original game."

But then, with the remaster almost completed and only 90 bugs left to fix, the project was cancelled after disputes between Microsoft (Rare's new overlord), Activision, Eon Productions, and Nintendo. Nintendo reportedly decided that they wanted *GoldenEye* to stay a Nintendo game for Nintendo platforms only—it was speculated that Nintendo president Satoru Iwata himself blocked the remaster's release. To make matters weirder, only a few years later, in 2010, Microsoft did successfully work things out with Nintendo to rerelease *Perfect Dark* on XBLA. The remaster runs at a faster, smoother frame rate, with improved graphics that preserve the original aesthetic; it even incorporated some *GoldenEye* shout-outs, including *GoldenEye* guns as well as multiplayer maps for Facility, Temple, and Complex. A second theory, then, for the scuttling of the remaster is that Eon Productions, license holders of all things James Bond, didn't appreciate how Bond was portrayed in the original *GoldenEye*—or that they didn't want to show Brosnan's face just as Daniel Craig was assuming the Bond mantle in 2008.

Insult was added to injury after Rare didn't include *GoldenEye* in their 2015 Rare Replay collection, a set of

30 games and making-of features dusted off from the vaults to celebrate the studio's 30th anniversary. When asked whether *GoldenEye*'s exclusion came down to licensing headaches, company reps said no, answering that they omitted it because they don't see *GoldenEye* as a pure Rare title since Rare didn't create the characters. Studio operations director Drew Quackenbush added that the game didn't fit other criteria as well. "We asked: Were they fun, how well have they aged, etc.," he said in 2015. "We wanted to bring in a broad range of games: popular games that would hit that nostalgic beat that everyone likes." Of course, this smelled like bullshit to most fans, considering that *GoldenEye* is one of Rare's most fun games of all time and certainly carries more fan nostalgia than *Digger T. Rock* (1990) or *R.C. Pro-Am 2* (1992), which did make the cut for the Replay collection.

The whole thing got even more suspicious after July 2019, when an anonymous former Rare employee leaked several professionally produced *GoldenEye* "making-of" videos that he said were originally intended for potential use in—you guessed it—Rare Replay. It seemed Rare had intended from the start to include *GoldenEye* in the Replay collection, until something went wrong. Were Nintendo, Activision, Eon, and Microsoft continuing to tangle over the rights to *GoldenEye*?

Fans finally got answers in February 2021, when YouTuber Graslu00 uploaded a two-hour walkthrough of the remastered *GoldenEye*, which he said he received from an anonymous party (undoubtedly a former Rare employee). Shortly thereafter, a fully playable, near-final beta version of the remaster, dated August 2007, was leaked. The ROM, which runs on PC emulators or modified Xbox hardware, is now widely available to download from social media posts, YouTube uploads, and Twitch streams. It's a beautiful remaster, loyal to the original but nicer to look at. It's also extremely fun to play with the Xbox's dual stick controllers. Guard faces have sadly been replaced, as has Dr. Doak, though some fans have already modified the ROM to add him back in. And if you beat the single-player campaign in the remaster, the very last line of the end credits reads, "BRING GE BACK, MGM/EON," implying its own story about who was to blame for the cancellation.

"The current excitement over the leak of this 'naughty remaster' speaks volumes for the impact and enduring legacy of *GoldenEye 007*," Doak told the BBC after the leak. But as of late 2021, neither Microsoft nor Rare nor Nintendo seem to want to claim *GoldenEye* as their own—or they're unable to due to ongoing licensing fights. None of the companies currently have any *GoldenEye* products listed in their company merchandise stores, and Rare often leaves *GoldenEye* out of their marketing art and their corporate mythology. *GoldenEye* isn't mentioned in their 35-year anniversary post and makes no appearance on the "Games" section of their website. The reason why Rare has orphaned one of their greatest hits of all time remains a mystery.

•

Only a month after the release of the critical and commercial failure *007 Legends* in 2012, the game's developer Eurocom—the studio behind seven Bond games including *GoldenEye* 2010—shut down completely. As of 2021, no Bond game has debuted since *Legends*, and for nearly a decade no game developer even held the license. The Bond video game franchise seemed dead and buried until IO Interactive, a Danish developer famous for creating the Hitman series, announced they'd be taking on the character for a game they're temporarily calling "Project 007." The game will feature a totally original Bond story with a brand-new Bond, and will play on consoles and PCs. IO CEO Hakan Abrak said that Barbara Broccoli, head of Eon Productions, swore that Bond wouldn't appear in another video game because previous Bond games weren't "worthy enough" and were too violent. But apparently she was sold on Abrak's pitch. Only time will tell whether IO's Bond game goes the way of all other Bond games since *GoldenEye*.

Then again, the future of *GoldenEye* may not lie with any particular company at all, but rather with talented amateur designers volunteering their time to keep the title alive with modern gamers. *GoldenEye: Source* is an open-source mod developed by a tightknit group of diehard fans who started rebuilding *GoldenEye*'s original multiplayer in Valve's Source engine (used for *Half-Life 2*) in 2005, just for the fun of it. After five years of development, the amateur developers had completed their high-definition PC port, and some commentators claimed it looked even better than the 2010 *GoldenEye*. In addition to recreating the original multiplayer maps, *GoldenEye: Source* offered new locations inspired by other Bond films. PC Gamer named *GoldenEye: Source* one of the top ten free fan remake classics, and Doak himself played *Source* online with the dev team to celebrate *GoldenEye*'s 20th anniversary.

The passion behind projects like *GoldenEye: Source* exemplifies a cultural nostalgia so profound that used N64 consoles and *GoldenEye* cartridges have seen a recent sales resurgence. eBay included the N64 in its 2019 holiday guide of "most-wanted gifts" for gamers, and Gamevaluenow.com estimates the value of a new, sealed copy of *GoldenEye* at $831.79, which speaks volumes about the preciousness of the object itself as a collectible remnant of the past. "Those consoles, which were the end of physical cartridges, are enjoying a second life as collectible things, and a lot of them still function," Doak told me. "You can't play *Fortnite* as it was a month ago—it's gone and they'll never switch it back to there, and even things that got physical distribution like *Last of Us* or *Red Dead* are discs and highly dependent on patches and updates and stuff. There is no canonical version of the game. With those N64 games, the cart is the game and everyone knows you're talking about exactly the same thing."

Used *GoldenEye* cartridges sell on eBay for as low as $70 in 2021, but if you're more of a retro-gamer than a retro-collector, you can also download the game ROM and play it on a PC emulator with a USB controller. Or you could buy an EverDrive, an N64 cartridge with an insertable SIM card that lets you load up and play hundreds of downloadable game ROMs on your original N64 console.

If you'd prefer new content—the true *GoldenEye* sequel you always longed for featuring the same game engine, art style, and Bond universe but a different story, mission objectives, and guns—then you can download fan-made mods, which are custom-built levels and even entire campaigns that use *GoldenEye*'s original graphics. *GoldenEye*'s extremely active modding community has been keeping the game alive for the past 25 years, and has a ton to offer the nostalgic *GoldenEye* fan.

The quality of the writing and level design in these mods can vary considerably, since everything is made by amateurs, but it's endlessly thrilling to see the original art assets recombined in new forms with new challenges for the player, and many mods are both beautifully designed and super fun to play. These mods vary from the silly, like the "Ken Lobb Classic," which forces players to complete the whole game using only the infamous Klobb, to the serious, like mods set in WWII and at Chernobyl.

The most famous *GoldenEye* mod by far, however, is *Goldfinger 64*, a 2017 campaign based on the Bond film *Goldfinger*. Many consider it the only "true" sequel to

GoldenEye, and N64 Today founder Martin Watts calls it a "triumph for the N64 modding community." A team of seventeen modders with code names like Monkeyface and Zoinkity put together the game over the course of more than six years with a precise attention to detail; the mod crew even talked to members of the original *GoldenEye* team for help. *Goldfinger 64* stars Sean Connery as Bond and takes place in Mexico, Miami, and the Swiss Alps. The game features twenty new levels (each much larger than *GoldenEye*'s), new weapons, new props, new character models, a new soundtrack, new sound effects, and eleven new multiplayer arenas. The use of the original *GoldenEye* engine, art assets, and mission structure—combined with all-new everything else—makes this game feel like a true sequel.

"*Goldfinger 64* reminds you what it was like to play *GoldenEye 007* for the first time," Watts writes in N64 Today. "This game captures the essence of what made *GoldenEye 007* so great and distils it into a brand new experience. If you're a fan of the original then you simply must play this game."

And if you want the true "sequel you've waited your whole life for" experience, you can even buy a *Goldfinger 64* cartridge online for $75 and plug it into your N64 console—a rare opportunity, since most mods simply run on PC emulators. The box art and sticker on the cartridge, based on original promotional posters for *Goldfinger*, look exactly like the game was really produced by Rare and Nintendo—it even has a "T" for teen rating on the cartridge.

The absence of a decent *GoldenEye* sequel might epitomize the cultural impact of the original. For a generation of gamers, *GoldenEye* represented a kind of religion—a group ritual played at parties and sleepovers, producing hours and hours of joy with friends. For a lot of players, *GoldenEye* marked a kind of rite of passage into adulthood. Our gaming careers began with Mario's cute Goombas but then shifted, during our teenage years, to *GoldenEye*'s Russian soldiers bleeding to death in a bunker. For console gamers, *GoldenEye* was the first FPS many of us ever played.

Now, *GoldenEye* is more than just a popular video game—it's a cultural touchstone with a cult following. *GoldenEye* distracted us from abusive parents and deep personal grief. It cemented our friendships and brought us closer with our siblings. *GoldenEye* still represents, for many of us, our most cherished childhood memories. "For my birthday one year," my friend Ben told me, "my Dad let us hook up the N64 to the church projector and sound system (on a Saturday) with all the Mountain Dew we could drink. It might be one of my favorite memories."

GoldenEye nostalgia, Watts told me, is "a memory of a time when [gaming] felt really magical."

Nearly 25 years after its release, *GoldenEye* still tops "best games of all time" lists, as well as lists of the best first-person shooters, best Nintendo games, and best

N64 games. It always tops the list of best games based on movies. In 2007, *GoldenEye* made *GamePro*'s list of "the 52 most important video games of all time," earning the title "the best console first-person shooter of all time," and in 2012, the Smithsonian American Art Museum decided to include *GoldenEye* in its 2012 "Art of Video Games" exhibit after a public vote on what games to feature. *GoldenEye* was even named one of twelve finalists for 2020 induction into the Strong Museum's World Video Game Hall of Fame in Rochester, New York.

Critics frequently discuss *GoldenEye*'s seismic impact on the gaming landscape. Writer Tom Bissell calls *GoldenEye* "the *Ulysses* of video games. It did everything a video game was capable of doing till that point, and it blasted open all these other avenues of possibility." *GoldenEye* helped bring the first-person shooter—formerly a PC-only genre—to a new audience of gamers by popularizing the genre on home consoles, essentially making first-person shooters mainstream. One critic sums up the influence this way: "No *GoldenEye 007*? No *Call of Duty*. It really is that simple."

"It proved to the industry and to consumers that it was a viable genre for home consoles," Watts told me. Because console-only gamers tended to be younger and less technologically savvy than PC gamers, *GoldenEye* made first-person shooters approachable for a whole new audience of gamers, which in turn expanded the entire genre.

GoldenEye also established many of the first-person shooter's common design features, including mission structure, multiplayer, gameplay, AI, and open-ended level architecture—all of which broke new ground in 1997, when the gaming landscape was full of cheap Doom clones. Since *GoldenEye*, almost all first-person shooters—both console- and PC-based—have taken something away from the game, whether directly or indirectly. *Thief: The Dark Project* (1998) built upon *GoldenEye*'s stealth mechanics, and *GoldenEye*'s pioneering approach to storytelling and realism influenced *Half-Life*, then *Medal of Honor* and *Call of Duty*. Today, the FPS console fire that *GoldenEye* ignited still blazes in franchises like Battlefield and Counter-Strike.

Even the term "first-person shooter" only came into wide use after *GoldenEye*. Before that, it was "3D adventure" or "*Doom* clone," but Google Usenet data shows that the phrase "*Doom* clone" dropped out of use after *GoldenEye*'s release and the term "first-person shooter" took off. Although *GoldenEye* ads didn't actually use this term, they did emphasize the idea of first-person, with phrasing like "you are Bond." In making the genre itself more mainstream, *GoldenEye* may have also precipitated the term "first-person shooter" into the common gaming lexicon.

If *GoldenEye* the film saved the Bond franchise, then *GoldenEye* the game solidified its enduring coolness. When *GoldenEye* the game debuted, it reinvigorated not only Bond-themed video games but Bond himself, acting as a kind of gateway drug to Bond fandom. "You play the game and you want to watch the movie, and you watch the movie and you want to watch other Brosnan Bond movies and then you go on and maybe you end up reading the Ian Fleming novels," *The World of GoldenEye* author Nicolás Suszczyk told me, emphasizing that *GoldenEye*'s overall legacy is about much more than the game alone. Still, exit polls after screenings of 1999's *The World Is Not Enough* indicated that Bond games had introduced Bond to a new generation of fans. And to this day, if you overhear someone say the word "*GoldenEye*," it's far more likely that they're talking about the game than the movie.

TOMORROW NEVER DIES

ONE DAY, AFTER *GOLDENEYE* had started to sell well, Tim Stamper called the Bond team into Rare's conference room for a surprise meeting.

"It's all going very well, lads," Stamper told them. "I bought you a little present." He held up a small red box containing an expensive Omega Seamaster watch—the Q-issued watch from *GoldenEye* the film that Doak had transformed into a laser weapon and pause screen in *GoldenEye* the game. Rare had bought a job lot of twelve of them, and at the time they each cost around £800 (£1,418 or $1,859 in 2021).

The rewards didn't end there. Rare's bonus structure at the time paid royalties based on a game's success and on how much a team member had contributed. "The royalty rate started at 17 cents a cartridge on *GoldenEye*," Kirkhope told Eurogamer in 2020, split between the team. Since *GoldenEye* sold eight million copies, would add up to at least £13,600 per team member, or £23,180 adjusted for inflation.

But more important than the financial rewards, as life-changing as they were for the young men, was the creative success of the game—the ways so many ordinary kids seemed to really love playing it. Their reputations at Rare had also drastically improved—maybe even too much. By March 1998, the *Banjo-Kazooie* team played *GoldenEye* every day at lunch, and on the archived Rare website from the era, one of the *GoldenEye* developers confessed that the game's success meant that "Everybody hates us now." Despite the joking tone of this comment, *GoldenEye*'s massive success did challenge the Stampers' secretive attitudes around the press.

"They had this kind of monolithic way of portraying the company," Doak said in 2017, "and then part of the company had done this thing that was really, really successful and was really important to the N64 and also kind of redefined the first-person shooter, so people wanted to talk to us about it." As they started giving interviews to journalists, several members of the team asked management, "How do our careers progress from here?" They wanted to do more than just start working on another game—they wanted to contribute to higher-level decisions about the direction of the company.

Fancy watches, in other words, weren't going to cut it for everyone. "We had ambitions beyond working every hour that God sends in the middle of nowhere to make other people rich," Doak told Nintendo Life. "After *GoldenEye*, it was very much, 'Well, we've laid a golden egg and you want us to lay another one, [so] what do we get? Other than waiting to see if we get a bonus?'"

The company's workaholic culture had started to frustrate some of the Bond team members, as did restrictive contracts and a feeling of unfair favoritism amongst the company. "Driving one hundred miles on a round trip to Twycross every day wasn't too much fun either," Ellis added.

And so, at the end of 1998, Doak made the tough decision to leave Rare, and Ellis, Norgate, and Hilton followed soon after. "At the time we were not popular for the decision," Hilton told Eurogamer.

When Ellis told the Stampers at 9 a.m. that he was leaving, he was booted out the door by 10:00 and had to call Edmonds later that afternoon to tie up some loose ends on *Perfect Dark*. "Anybody leaving their company, [the Stamper brothers] would take it personally," Hollis mused in 2020. "The reason they take it personally is that they've invested so much of their own personality into the making of that company. From that position, it's like it's a personal insult."

After their exodus from Rare, Doak, Ellis, Norgate, and Hilton created their own game development company called Free Radical. They did not start the new project with their former mentors' blessing. "I remember sitting in an office with Tim and Chris, and Tim telling me I would fail," Doak told Eurogamer. "My exit meeting was that, was being given a last chance to recant, and Tim saying to me, 'When Chris and I set something up, it wasn't as hard as it is now. And I think you'll find it's going to be really hard and you won't succeed.'"

But while going independent felt incredibly daunting, Norgate said later, it was "also amazingly exciting too [...] It was not a decision I took lightly. [...] In fact, the morning I left Rare, I went back to a colleague's house, drank whiskey, and shook from head to toe wondering what the hell I'd just let myself into. Luckily, the next ten years were a decade I'll never forget."

In its heyday, Free Radical was highly respected as an innovative and high-quality game developer. Ellis noted the joys of Free Radical's early days, when the team stayed small and the possibilities felt limitless. "You didn't have to justify it to a publisher, you didn't have to write it all down on paper, you didn't have a committee of people looking at it, chang[ing] it and decid[ing] if it's a rubbish idea," Ellis said in 2012. "You could come up with an idea in the morning and have it running by the afternoon and decide if it's any good by actually trying it out. That's a good environment for making games."

Free Radical's first project was *TimeSplitters* (2000), a first-person shooter that experimented with all the things Doak, Ellis, and Hilton had wanted to try in *GoldenEye* but couldn't: a faster frame rate, a lighter tone, a wider range of characters, more diverse environments, and a mapmaker. "*GoldenEye*, because it's the Bond universe—particularly the Bond universe from that one film—is incredibly narrow in its scope, in terms of environments and characters," Doak said in 2018, but now the team could innovate to their hearts' content. Unfortunately, publishers didn't always make this easy. Early on, Free Radical had rocky relationships with publishers who didn't know how to market a goofy, cartoony first-person shooter. The humor that had worked so well for them with *GoldenEye* was now a liability.

Ultimately, *TimeSplitters*, *TimeSplitters 2* (2002), and a third title, *Second Sight* (2004) sold well and received critical acclaim. But after these early successes, Free Radical hit trouble working with EA on a third TimeSplitters title—*TimeSplitters Future Perfect* (2005). According to Ellis, EA told Free Radical they didn't plan to market Future Perfect, prioritizing all their attention instead on—ironically—*GoldenEye: Rogue Agent*. "We killed ourselves getting *Future Perfect* done," Doak said later, "only to find that they had made a total balls of [*GoldenEye: Rogue Agent*] to the extent they had to throw more money at it to market it—the money that they might have spent on *Future Perfect*. I mean, it's like fiction that it's a *GoldenEye* game, isn't it? I don't think the irony of what they were doing ever occurred to EA."

Free Radical's next project, *Haze* (2008), was a fascinating psychological first-person shooter with an anti-war concept at its heart and innovative approaches to story and gameplay. But unfortunately, it ended up being Free Radical's last game. After endless problems working with Ubisoft, Sony, and LucasArts on Haze—and particularly with LucasArts on *Star Wars: Battlefront III* and *IV*—Free Radical thought it had been saved when Activision approached them in 2008 suggesting they could work on the *GoldenEye* 2010 remake. Much to the heartbreak of the former GoldenEye team members, though, the deal was never finalized, and the project ended up going to Eurocom. It seems obvious that if you want to make a Bond game as successful as *GoldenEye*, you should work with the people who made *GoldenEye*, but apparently Activision didn't see it that way—and paid the price, ultimately, with all the Bond flops they produced between 2006 and 2013.

All in all, Free Radical became overwhelmed by pressures from an industry trending away from innovation and risk-taking in favor of safe profit margins. Doak has said in several interviews that he's annoyed about the ways that publishers can alter a designer's vision by trying to play it too safe, and that brand IP development and "sequelitis" destroys creativity. "I've grown over the years to just detest that," he said in 2018. "Ever since I've left the mainstream industry, I've just watched AAA games become narrower and narrower in scope and ambition […] and it's just shameful." In 2009, Free Radical was purchased by German game developer Crytek, who eventually closed in 2014 and transferred its staff to a new studio called Dambuster, whose parent company was Deep Silver.

Around the same time that Free Radical's founders left Rare, Hollis called it quits, too. "The management structure was in place and there wasn't anywhere for me to go once I'd reached the level I reached," Hollis told IGN. He wanted new challenges, and he didn't want to get stuck making one first-person-shooter after another for the rest of his career. And so, a little over a year into development of *Perfect Dark*, Hollis left Rare. "It's a difficult moment to leave a team that you love and a game that you love," Hollis said in another interview, "but I did feel that at that point the project was no longer exciting to me, and I think the reason for that was that it was too similar to *GoldenEye*." Leaving Rare was painful, Hollis told me. "It was not a smooth break," he said. "I was midway through a four-year fixed term contract, but I couldn't agree with management's ultimatum that I sign a new four-year contract immediately. I wanted to stay and finish *Perfect Dark*. But in retrospect I am so glad I didn't stay for another long project."

After a six-month trip around south Asia and a stint in Washington working for Nintendo of America on the development of the GameCube console, Hollis moved to Cambridge and established Zoonami, a game development company he ran for the next ten years with a mission to make "original games with original verbs and original game mechanics pushing new directions while working with traditional publishers." By 2004, Hollis had a core staff of seven as well as many contractors. The company focused on innovation—taking chances, pushing game genres, and inventing new genres entirely. One such game, *Bonsai Barber*, was released in 2009 for the Wii, involved giving haircuts to adorable cartoon trees—a far cry from the bloody violence of *GoldenEye*.

After ten years, Hollis closed Zoonami because he wanted a change and a break.

The *GoldenEye* team developed the best game of their era by innovating and experimenting. They took this mindset with them into their next ventures, but the industry kept constricting them as it changed. "I've been making games for so long that I'm no longer interested in the pure and simple goal, which should be respected, of just making a good game," Hollis said in 2010. "I'm more interested in […] trying to push the field. Increasingly I feel the games that get made are typically from a fairly narrow set of possibilities, and I feel there's an incredible range of possible games that could be made. Most people aren't really exploring that, and that's what really excites me. The Wild West—no one's even there yet. The real blue ocean of game design is what excites me most."

•

General turnover at Rare had always been so low that the company was a bit shaken up after the *GoldenEye* team's mini-exodus. They had to pull the plug on *Killer Instinct 3* because so many members of its team had to fill in the new vacancies on *Perfect Dark*. Still, Rare was riding so high after *GoldenEye*'s success that it moved to a multi-million-dollar new facility in 1999.

But then, in 2002, Nintendo sold its entire stake in Rare to Microsoft, ending Nintendo's twenty-year relationship with Rare and changing the developer forever. Microsoft and Rare fundamentally disagreed about which games to make and how to make them—Rare worked well with the light-hearted, childlike tone of Japanese games while Microsoft wanted macho, American-style games for the Xbox. "Microsoft and Rare was a bad marriage from the beginning," Hollis mused in 2012. "The groom was rich. The bride was beautiful." After the Microsoft buyout, the culture at Rare became stricter and more stressful, and many of Rare's staff felt smothered. Microsoft didn't seem to trust Rare to take direction over their own projects, and the development environment became stifled by constant meetings and performance reviews. The resulting games were mediocre at best. In the end, the Microsoft merger only revealed how crucial Nintendo's gentle influence and generous freedom had been to Rare's earlier successes.

During *GoldenEye*'s development years, "we were basically an indie team making a AAA product," Doak said later—a phenomenon that would be basically impossible today, when massive studios focus increasingly on flashy graphics than on revolutionary new gameplay mechanics.

GoldenEye marked "a transitional moment," game design scholar Stefan Hall told me, where "small development groups were able to produce very polished titles that really engage the player, and then the drive started becoming, much like in the film industry: bigger hits, more spectacle, more sensation, more attraction."

•

As of 2021, the original *GoldenEye* team members are now scattered around the UK, the US, and Canada. Martin Hollis remains passionate about games—in particular, games that no one has ever invented before. In 2013, he presented a matchmaking game called *Aim for Love* —a deviation, he said, from a constant stream of games about guns, shooting, and war. At the 2012 Game Developers Conference, Hollis told a packed audience: "Games have been about war for thousands of years. Why not change that? Really, my message is an old message for a new industry: Make love games, not war games. And, maybe, in 5,000 years, half of the games will be about war. And half about love."

Mark Edmonds stayed at Rare for twenty years. After Hollis left Rare, he took over as project lead for *Perfect Dark*, and by all accounts did an excellent job. After *Perfect Dark*, he worked on some unreleased game prototypes—including an MMORPG, a fantasy game, and a space shooter—and then on *Perfect Dark Zero*, a 2005 Xbox 360 prequel to *Perfect Dark*. Today, he works for Smilegate Barcelona, a Korean company that makes *CrossFire*, the most-played video game in the world according to total player count. He seems tickled to be back working on a first-person shooter after that's how his whole career began.

Karl Hilton is the studio director at Lockwood, a game company that produces *Avakin Life*, a 3D social networking virtual world with a little more than a million daily users. He loves working on a live service, and he's always charmed when users dress up their avatars in tuxedos for James Bond film releases. He still meets people at parties who ask him to sign their *GoldenEye* cartridge boxes.

Brett Jones makes 3D models for TV and films these days, including *Dr. Who*, *Guardians of the Galaxy*, *The Mummy*, *Fantastic Beasts and Where to Find Them*, and *The Fast and the Furious*, among others. He is currently previsualization asset supervisor on an Amazon adaptation of *Anansi Boys* by Neil Gaimon. His biggest passion, though, is the Sci-Fi Ball, an annual three-day convention that has been running for 25 years now. In addition to directing and emceeing the entire event, Jones puts his epic knowledge of sci-fi geekery to use in the event's charity auction, which is also part basically a stand-up comedy routine. Doak recently attended the Sci-Fi Ball and loved seeing Jones in his element as emcee, egging people on to buy commemorative *Star Trek* plates and causing Doak to spit out his beer laughing when he referred to Edmonds offhandedly by his old nickname "The Length."

Duncan Botwood still wears his Omega Seamaster watch every day. He continued his motion capture and voice-acting career in several other games, including *Star Fox Adventures* (2002), in which he voiced the villain Andross. Today, Botwood serves as an associate level design director at Ubisoft and lives in Toronto. He's worked on *Splinter Cell: Blacklist*, *Assassin's Creed: Unity*, and *Far Cry Primal*. Younger co-workers still approach Botwood around the office to share their favorite *GoldenEye* memories with him. And although Botwood lives quite far from his former colleagues, he still occasionally sees them—Doak recently grabbed beers with him during a trip to Canada.

Today, Ady Smith is a game art lecturer at Falmouth University, where he's passionate about making games education less academic and more hands-on—the kind of education he needed himself as an artistic youth who struggled in school. "You don't do it for the money," he told me. "You do it for the feedback that you get from the students." He's especially proud of getting his first student into the industry. His career—which started with recruiting, training, and teaching new Rare employees—has come full circle.

David Doak lives in rural Norfolk now, where he raises his teenage daughters and teaches at Norwich University of the Arts. In his free time, he teaches young children in after-school clubs how to make Lego robots. "I think that's probably one of the ways I'm most likely to influence the future of video games, is to spark a fire in someone else," he said in 2016. On Twitter, "Dr. Doak" keeps *GoldenEye* fandom alive, posting hilarious memes and congratulating speedrunners when they break new records. He's also back in the lab again, working on virtual reality techniques for modeling protein structures just like he did back in his pre-Rare and pre-*GoldenEye* days.

Ken Lobb is a creative director at Microsoft, where he continues to make games with the same passion and excitement he did at Nintendo and Rare. "I am a HUGE Halo fan, as are many of the readers here, and most Xbox owners," Lobb said in an interview with Mundorare. "However, I also have a large place in my heart for *GoldenEye* (the real one [smiles]), and *Perfect Dark*."

Today, Steve Ellis enjoys regular *Fortnite* sessions between himself, his son, and Doak—a kind of proxy, during COVID times, for meeting down at the pub. After working for eight years in iOS game development, Ellis took on a "secret role" with Deep Silver, the company that bought the company that bought Free Radical Design Ltd, the studio he'd founded with Norgate, Hilton, and Doak. Then, in May 2021, *TimeSplitters* fans went wild with the news that Free Radical—13 years after it went bankrupt—was being re-formed by Deep Silver as the first steps of reviving the TimeSplitters franchise. At the helm of the studio are none other than Ellis and Doak.

Grant Kirkhope lives with his wife and kids in LA, where he works as a freelance composer. Over the course of his career, he's composed many iconic soundtracks, including *Perfect Dark*, *Donkey Kong 64*, Banjo-Kazooie, *Super Smash Bros. Ultimate*, *Yooka-Laylee*, and *Viva Piñata*. He recently worked on *The King's Daughter*, a live-action movie starring Pierce Brosnan. "It's funny, I'm writing for Pierce Brosnan again after writing for him with *GoldenEye* back in the day," Kirkhope told *Game Informer*. Since moving to America, Kirkhope has become a US citizen and debuted his first concert piece, a delightful trombone concerto called "Kirkfeld" that you can find on Spotify. As of early 2021, he was composing the score for *Bringing Back GoldenEye*, the sequel to the mockumentary *Going for GoldenEye*, and remains deeply grateful to be where he is today: "Sometimes I think to myself, 'I can't believe I'm making a living writing music—I don't know how it's possible,'" Kirkhope told me.

After *GoldenEye*, Graeme Norgate went on to compose music for *Diddy Kong Racing* (1997), *Jet Force Gemini* (1999), and *Perfect Dark* (2000) before leaving for Free Radical Design. Today, he's a senior audio director at Lockwood Publishing working alongside Hilton. As the industry progressed, Norgate found himself in more management-focused roles than creatively-oriented ones, which he didn't like—"I almost get anxious if I don't make stuff," he told me. But now that he's in mobile gaming, things feel more like the old days again. "I'm still doing what I've always wanted to do which is write music for games," he told me.

Though they're spread across every corner of the globe, *GoldenEye*'s team members still all keep in touch. "Because we were so young and everyone was working so hard, those bonds are quite deep" Norgate told me.

During the COVID quarantine in the spring of 2020, some of the old Rare employees started meeting up on Zoom for curry night every few weeks. "We're older now, we've got mortgages and wives [and kids], but it's not very different," Kirkhope told me—even

25 years later, the "curry boys" still bring up the same old jokes and tease each other the same old ways. In a recent photo of some of the guys posted to Twitter, they all toast to the camera with their drinks of choice: at least one Strongbow and beers of varying hue. They look happy to be together again, even if their visit is mediated through a screen. Fun on a screen, after all, is what brought them together in the first place.

NOTES

THIS BOOK IS THE RESULT of dozens of hours of interviews and a breadth of research across games journalism, cultural criticism, academic sources, and popular writing. This section includes both sources which informed the writing of this book as a whole, followed by chapter-specific references.

Articles:

"'I Didn't Really Know What I Was Working On': How Nine People at Rare Created a Seminal Classic with *GoldenEye*" in GamesRadar (2018): https://bit.ly/2Bsgrys; James Berardinelli's "Review: *Goldeneye*" in Reelviews.net (1995): https://bit.ly/2M9qPRM; Jon Jordan's "The Restless Vision of Martin Hollis, the Man with the *GoldenEye*" in Game Developer [formerly Gamasutra] (2007): https://ubm.io/31q1iYE; Elliot Figueira's "N64: 20 Hidden Details in *GoldenEye 007* Real Fans Completely Missed" in Screen Rant (2019): https://bit.ly/2Bi383s; Benjamin Svetkey's "Is James Bond Still a Big Gun?" in *Entertainment Weekly* (1995): https://bit.ly/314gIBW; Jeremy Glass's "10 Things You Didn't Know About *GoldenEye* N64" in Thrillist (2015): https://bit.ly/31l3b93; Quinn Myers's "An Oral History of *GoldenEye 007* on the N64" in MEL Magazine (2018): https://bit.

ly/31dv2b9; Paul Drury's "The Making of Goldeneye" in Now Gamer (2011): https://bit.ly/368X6Qt; "The Making of Goldeneye" in *NGC Magazine* (issue 60, 2001); "GoldenEye" in *Retro Gamer UK* (issue 178, 2018); "The Golden Touch–*Edge* Interviews the Goldeneye 007 Team" in *Edge* (1997): https://bit.ly/2SFOZH5; Mike Rougeau's "Is Miyamoto Really Responsible For Unrealistic Dual-Wielding in Games?" in Kotaku (2013): https://bit.ly/2W4lkHq; Justin Woo's "The 10 Most Influential Games in History" in Game Crate (2017); Alberto Riol, A. Fernánez, and Iker Pérez's "The Men Who Knew Too Much" in MundoRare; Alberto Riol, A. Fernánez, and Iker Pérez's "K. Lobb Shoots and Gets Shot!" in MundoRare; "Box Office History for James Bond Movies" in The Numbers: https://bit.ly/355LY6I; Wesley Yin-Poole's "*Perfect Dark*: The Oral History of an N64 Classic" in Eurogamer (2020): https://bit.ly/2GZUkWh; James Proctor's "Original *GoldenEye 007* Producer Would Love To Be Involved In Remake" in Gaming Bible (2020): https://bit.ly/2LZjumF; Mark James Hardisty's "James Bond Q&A: Karl Hilton (@KarlHilton1) and Tony Wills" (2016): https://bit.ly/2rKIU16; *CRASH* magazine (issue 51, 1988): https://bit.ly/365OgC7; "Former Nintendo Exec Ken Lobb on *GoldenEye 007*'s Rail Shooter Origins, Klobb Gun, More" in Nintendo Everything (2017): https://bit.ly/39n4SZ7; Simon Parkin's "Who Killed Rare?" in Eurogamer (2012): https://bit.ly/3bH1J7i; Mark Walbank's "Creative Minds" in Computer and Video Games (2007): https://bit.ly/3bO-lES6; "Desert Island Disks: David Doak" in Retro Gamer (issue 6, 2004): https://bit.ly/2U78ZmL; Nathan Birch's "The Multiplayer Mode Was Made in a Month? 12 Killer Facts About the N64 Classic *GoldenEye 007*" in Uproxx (2015): https://bit.ly/2zbfM2X; "Rare Vintage" in Edge (2010): https://bit.ly/3gW54Cg; Keith Stuart and Jordan Erica Webber's "*GoldenEye* on N64: Miyamoto Wanted to

Tone Down the Killing" in the *Guardian* (2015): https://bit.
ly/2MXbMtn; "Duncan Botwood Interviewed" in The RWP
(2008): https://bit.ly/2ZBFD0B; "GameCube Developer
Profile: Rare" in IGN (2001): https://bit.ly/37xVwYP; Sam
Shahrani's "Educational Feature: A History and Analysis of
Level Design in 3D Computer Games" in Game Developer
(2006): https://ubm.io/2nziY62; James Batchelor's "*Perfect
Dark* Turns 20–The Definitive Story Behind the N64 Hit
that Outclassed James Bond" in Nintendo Life (2020):
https://bit.ly/2JZe8du; James Willcox's "The Name of
the Game is 64 Bits" in Popular Mechanics (1996); Rus
McLaughlin's "IGN Presents the History of Rare" in IGN
(2008): https://bit.ly/2vxoiec; "A Rare Breed" in *Retro Gamer*
(issue 20): https://bit.ly/36cMMpX; Michael Krantz's "64
Bits of Magic" in *Time* (1996): https://bit.ly/2HkbXwB;
"The Rare Essentials" in *N64 Magazine* (issue 13, 1998); "20
Years Later: The History of *Goldeneye 007* N64" in Teechu
(2017): https://bit.ly/2VRaVP2; "10 *GoldenEye* Facts"
YouTube video (2015): https://bit.ly/2W67DI0; Daniel
Vuckovic's "Remembering *Goldeneye 007* with Former
Rareware Lead Artist Karl Hilton" in Vooks (2017): https://
bit.ly/2ZyCrCZ; Shaun McInnis's "The *GoldenEye 007* that
Never Was" in GameSpot (2012): https://bit.ly/2J3OH7g;
Meghan Flannery's "*GoldenEye*: The Quest to Re-Invent the
Video Game Standard" in How They Got Game" (2002):
https://stanford.io/3z75CPk; James Newton's "Rare Reveals
Nintendo Wanted to Cancel GoldenEye" in Nintendo Life
(2010): https://bit.ly/2thS9Gc; Jeff Gerstmann's "*GoldenEye
007* Review" in GameSpot (1997): https://bit.ly/2Bi5W0x;
Janet Burns's "15 Deadly Facts About *GoldenEye 007*" in
Mental Floss (2015): https://bit.ly/2BnS44E; Ryan Rigney's
"Nintendo 64's Music Maestro Unleashes His Hit Chiptunes
for Free" in *Wired* (2013): https://bit.ly/2BnKGqb; Amelia
Tait's "What Happened to All the Video Games Based on

Movies?" in New Statesman (2017): https://bit.ly/2XxhWYR; *Next Generation* (May 1997): https://bit.ly/2LNWlEP; Aaron Curtiss's "A Brainy Workout, and a Licence to Thrill" in the *Los Angeles Times* (1997): https://bit.ly/2AAgxXr; Adam Wakelin Hinckley's "Software Firm's 'Oscars' Triumph" in *Leicester Mercury* (1998); Gerald Voorhees's "Online First-Person Shooter Games" in *The International Encyclopedia of Digital Communication and Society* (2015); Daniel Stransky's "The Evolution of First-Person Shooter" in Culture of Gaming (2018): https://bit.ly/2obGF4E; Harper Jay MacIntyre's "That Time An Island In *GoldenEye* Disappointed A Generation" in Kotaku (2018): https://bit.ly/2VWKtU7; Carl Therrien's "Inspecting Video Game Historiography Through Critical Lens: Etymology of the First-Person Shooter Genre" in *Game Studies* (2015): https://bit.ly/2v8gLxo; Eric-Jon Rössel Waugh's "A Short History of Rare" in Bloomberg (2006): https://bit.ly/2UURIhc; David Lloyd, Ili Butterfield, and Larry Oji's "Composer Interview: Grant Kirkhope" in OverClocked ReMix (2008): https://bit.ly/2Fjhgvr; James Nouch's "Crash Lab's Steve Ellis on the Simple, Flexible, Creative Joys of Making iOS Games" in Pocket Gamer.biz (2012): https://bit.ly/37rid0H; Dan Pearson's "Zoonami Keeper" in Games Industry.biz (2010): https://bit.ly/2QxzHBz; Daniel Major's "Best Of 2019: GoldenEye Dev David Doak On Shaking (And Stirring) The FPS Genre On Console" in Nintendo Life (2019): https://bit.ly/2ZBI2bB; Jeff Alexander and Tom Bissell's "'Everything or Nothing" in Salon (2004): https://bit.ly/2pEMYhK; Chris Greening's "Graeme Norgate Interview: Composer of *GoldenEye* and *TimeSplitters*" in VGM (2011): https://bit.ly/2ZBDNg8; Chris Greening's "Interview with Grant Kirkhope" in Square Enix Music Online (2010): https://bit.ly/2sy5TwJ; Matt Martin's "The Collapse of Free Radical Design" in Games Industry.biz (2012): https://bit.ly/2tlthxl; "Time To Split: The Life and Death of the Free

Radicals" in Medium (2016): https://bit.ly/2QwEzHg; Matt Casamassina's "Interview: Martin Hollis" in IGN (2004): https://bit.ly/356XXQd; Wesley Yin-Poole's "The Man Who Made *GoldenEye*" in Eurogamer (2010): https://bit.ly/2MJn-QPT; Zak Wojnar's "From *GoldenEye* To *Yooka-Laylee*: Grant Kirkhope Reflects On His Career" in Game Informer (2017): https://bit.ly/2MKWQj0; "Dr. Doak Ask Me Anything" on Reddit (2020): https://bit.ly/3ebWpt3; "Nintendo, Virgin Latest to Take Developer Stakes" in *Consumer Multimedia Report* (1995); Ed Smith's "Mission Imperfection: A Love Letter to *GoldenEye 007*" in Vice (2015): https://bit.ly/2oNfDS5; Simon Parkin's "From Me to Wii: Martin Hollis' Journey" in Game Developer (2009): https://ubm.io/37oxhMy; and Simon Parkin's "Shooters: How Video Games Fund Arms Manufacturers" in Eurogamer (2019): https://bit.ly/2tgJiFb.

Books:

Katie Whitlock, Gerald Voorhees, and Joshua Call's *Guns, Grenades, and Grunts: First-Person Shooter Video Games* (Bloomsbury, 2012); Math Manent's *Nintendo 64 Anthology* (Diamond Comic Distributors, Inc., 2016); James Chapman's *License to Thrill: A Cultural History of the James Bond Films* (I.B. Tauris, 2007); Nicolás Suszczyk's *The World of GoldenEye* (2019); Christoph Lindner's *The James Bond Phenomenon: A Critical Reader* (Manchester University Press, 2009); James Egan's *3000 Facts About Video Games* (2015); Osamu Inoue's *Nintendo Magic: Winning the Videogame Wars* (Vertical, 2010); Daniel Sloan's *Playing to Wiin: Nintendo and the Video Game Industry's Greatest Comeback* (John Wiley & Sons, 2011); Jonathan Hennessey's *The Comic Book Story of Video Games: The Incredible History of the Electronic Gaming Revolution* (Ten Speed Press, 2017); Robert Mejia and Jaime

Banks's *100 Greatest Video Game Franchises* (Rowman & Littlefield, 2017); and Bill Loguidice's *Vintage Game Consoles: An Inside Look at Apple, Atari, Commodore, Nintendo, and the Greatest Gaming Platforms of All Time* (Routledge, 2017).

Websites:

"*GoldenEye* Rumour Mill" on Rare website: https://bit.ly/37fa1Am; GoldenEye: Decoded: https://goldeneyedecoded.blogspot.com; the Rare Archived Website: https://bit.ly/39tucvC; "*GoldenEye 007*" on The Cutting Room Floor: https://bit.ly/2MOaP6U; Rare Tepid Seat: https://bit.ly/3th3yQB; and Graham Douglas's GoldeneyeForever.com.

Videos:

"The Making of *GoldenEye 007* on N64 (parts 1 and 2)" (2019): https://bit.ly/2Q6gDvk; "*GoldenEye*: The Complete History" (2019): https://bit.ly/3tbOXFT; "The Retro Hour - Episode 19 (*GoldenEye* 64 and Rare with David Doak)" (2016): https://bit.ly/369EsrI; "The Composer Behind *GoldenEye 007, Banjo-Kazooie,* and More" (2017): https://bit.ly/2Qtrhva; Martin Hollis's "The Making of *GoldenEye 007*" presentation at the 2004 European Developer's Forum; "CPRE2 - Martin Hollis" presentation (2013); "*GoldenEye 007*: A Rare Retrospective" (2016): https://bit.ly/2P3rTbO; "David Doak - *GoldenEye007* - Do You Expect Me to Talk?" (2017): https://bit.ly/3exuFT5; Martin Hollis's "Classic Postmortem: *GoldenEye 007*" presentation at the 2012 Game Developers Conference: https://bit.ly/2oHWdho; "You Probably Shot This Man… (When Playing an N64) ft. Dr David Doak" (2019): https://bit.ly/2QtKsox; "*Goldeneye 007* (N64) - Did You Know Gaming?" (2013): https://bit.ly/37oGVyO; "*Goldeneye 007* (N64) - The Game that Changed the *Doom* Clone" (2017): https://bit.ly/2J-5D2oI; "DF Retro: Rare's N64 Classics - *GoldenEye* and *Perfect Dark*" (2016): https://bit.ly/2MuGvPz; "*Goldeneye* Developers Commentary 1 - WiiDS@GameCity" three-part video (2008): https://bit.ly/354qZzX, https://bit.ly/3besJLh, and https://bit.ly/3bh7DMf; "Martin Designs a Game - Martin Hollis" (2016): https://bit.ly/2ZyCbE1; "The Legacy of *GoldenEye 007*: Design Dive" (2019): https://bit.ly/38zIpJg; Tommy Thompson's "The AI of *GoldenEye 007*" in Game Developer (2019): https://bit.ly/2VjOxyc; "GameCity 3: *GoldenEye 007* Commentary with Martin Hollis and David Doak" (2008): https://bit.ly/368Rndp; "GI Show – The Nintendo 64 Spectacular Featuring Grant Kirkhope and Mega64" (2015): https://bit.ly/2tg4E5a; "David Doak Interview (*TimeSplitters, GoldenEye 64* & *Perfect Dark*) - The Cyber Den" (2019): https://bit.ly/369h25I; *Electric Playground* season 1 episode 3 (1997); "The Complete History of *GoldenEye 007*" (2018): https://bit.ly/2VPl26U; "*GoldenEye 007* - 15 Year Retrospective Review" (2012): https://bit.ly/2J8X8hJ; "David Doak (Creator of *TimeSplitters*)" (2018): https://bit.ly/2rCVlvJ; and IGS Podcast episode 58 "Grant Kirkhope" (2018): https://bit.ly/2ZEdIx3.

Other Sources:

"David Doak Interview" on *Arcade Attack* podcast (2020): https://bit.ly/3d3VZ7U; Stefan Hall's "'You've Seen the Movie, Now Play the Video Game': Recoding the Cinematic in Digital Media and Virtual Culture" PhD dissertation (2011); David Doak Twitter; and "Grant Kirkhope (*Banjo Kazooie*) Composer Interview" on Composer Code podcast (episode 16, 2019): https://bit.ly/353BaVn.

The following sources are organized by the chapters whose content they inform.

Mission Briefing

N64 Magazine (issue 7, Oct. 1997).

Killer Instincts and a Swagger

FPS statistics: Entertainment Software Association's "Essential Facts About the Computer and Video Game Industry (2017): https://bit.ly/32BIAnl.

Rare history: Steven Kent's *The Ultimate History of Video Games: From Pong to Pokemon—The Story Behind the Craze that Touched Our Lives and Changed the World* (Three Rivers Press, 2001); Candice Goodwin's "In Search of the Ultimate Game" in *Home Computing Weekly Magazine* (1983): https://bit.ly/2v37RWQ; "Retroview – *Knightlore*" in *Edge* (1994); Roger Kean and Nik Wild's "Ultimately Playing a Rare Game" in *The Games Machine* (1988): https://bit.ly/2TBQJ4H; David Kelly's "The Gang of Four" in *Popular Computing Weekly* (1983): https://bit.ly/362IH7n; Jimmy Maher's "The Legend of Ultimate Play the Game" in The Digital Antiquarian (2014): https://bit.ly/37bs1vO; Rebecca Levene and Magnus Anderson's *Grand Thieves & Tomb Raiders: How British Video Games Conquered the World* (Aurum Press, 2012); Heidi Dawley's "Killer Instinct for Hire" in Bloomberg (1995): https://bloom.bg/2uDo05B;

and "75 Power Players" in *Next Generation* (1995): https://bit.ly/2UOONGJ.

Early *GoldenEye* development: David Hancock's "The Name's Bond...DONKEY BOND" in the *Daily Mirror* (1995); *Nintendo Power* (vol. 71, 1995); and Martin Hollis's Twitter account.

Bond history: Tony Bennett and Janet Woollacott's *Bond and Beyond: The Political Career of a Popular Hero* (Routledge, 1987); J. McCollam's "25 Hidden Things Only Super Fans Know About *GoldenEye 007*" in TheGamer (2018): https://bit.ly/33J5VPg; Geoffrey Hellman's "James Bond Comes to New York" in *The New Yorker* (1962): https://bit.ly/2NosiDt; David Doak's "Hello Reddit": https://bit.ly/2ZuRwY1; and Ansh Patel's "Imperialism in the Worlds and Mechanics of First-Person Shooters" in *Journal of Games Criticism* (2016): https://bit.ly/2lZiOV8.

A View to a Game

Jessica Aldred's "*Tomb Raider*: Transmedia" In *How to Play Video Games* (2019); "*GoldenEye 007*" on Nintendo.com (1997): https://bit.ly/33GPm6I; and Tim Weaver's "Heads, You Lose" in *Arcade* (issue 20, 2000).

You Know the Name. You Know the Number.

***GoldenEye* movie history:** Owen Williams's "The Complete History of *GoldenEye*'s Opening Sequence" in Empire (2015): https://bit.ly/37lICwJ; Phil Pirrello's "'*GoldenEye*': 20 Things You (Probably) Didn't Know About the James Bond Classic" in Moviefone (2015): https://bit.ly/39ng1bq; Rogerebert.

com; Jim Leach's "'The World Has Changed': Bond in the 1990s—and Beyond?" in *The James Bond Phenomenon: A Critical Reader* (Manchester University Press, 2009); "From Russia with Scorn of Past Idols" in The Moscow Times (1996): https://bit.ly/2LNzA3F; Martin Willis's "Hard-Wear: The Millennium, Technology, and Brosnan's Bond" in *The James Bond Phenomenon: A Critical Reader*; Rich Watts's "*GoldenEye*" in Not Coming (2005): https://bit.ly/354hstT; James Kendrick's "*Goldeneye*" in Qnetwork.com: https://bit.ly/35rhmga; Christopher Null's "*Goldeneye*" in Filmcritic. com (1995): https://bit.ly/329zoBu; Richard von Busack's "Bond for Glory" in Metro Active (1995): https://bit.ly/2oWFLJy; "*GoldenEye* Set Reports" on YouTube (2018): https://bit.ly/2ZwXo14; "Behind the Scenes with Pierce Brosnan as James Bond 007" on YouTube (2010): https://bit.ly/2ZwXHZM; "*Goldeneye* News" in Klast (2006): https://bit.ly/2qb0Alp; "Film 95 Location Report - *Goldeneye*" YouTube video (1995): https://bit.ly/31ciiS8; and "*GoldenEye* on Set" YouTube video (2019): https://bit.ly/2F6nLBm.

License to Kill

FPS history: Matteo Bittanti's "From GunPlay to GunPorn: A Techno-Visual History of the First-Person Shooter" (2006); David McGowan's "Some of This Happened to the Other Fellow: Remaking *GoldenEye 007* with Daniel Craig" in *Game on, Hollywood! Essays on the Intersection of Video Games and Cinema*, ed. by Gretchen Papazian and Joseph Michael Sommers (McFarland and Company, 2013); Mark J.P. Wolf's "*BioShock Infinite*: World-Building" in *How to Play Video Games*, ed. by Matthew Thomas Payne and Nina B. Huntemann (New York University Press, 2019); Karen Collins's "Game Sound in the Mechanical Arcades: An

Audio Archaeology" in *Game Studies* (2016): https://bit.ly/2oWUNQd; Brooke Belisle's "Immersion" in *Debugging Game History: A Critical Lexicon*, ed. by Henry Lowood and Raiford Guins (MIT Press, 2016); "A 43-Year History of First-Person Shooters—from *Maze War* to *Destiny 2*" in GamesRadar (2017): https://bit.ly/2m54muY; Chris Kohler's *Power-Up: How Japanese Video Games Gave the World an Extra Life* (Courier Dover Publications, 2016); "Gaming's Most Important Evolutions" in GamesRadar (2010): https://bit.ly/2obiX8B; Daniel Engber's "Who Made That First-Person Shooter Game?" in the *New York Times* (2014): https://nyti.ms/2ohD4Cp; Marc Laidlaw's "The Egos at Id" in *Wired* (1996); David Kushner's *Masters of Doom: How Two Guys Created an Empire and Transformed Pop Culture* (Random House, 2004); and Jacob Gaboury's "Perspective" in *Debugging Game History*.

GoldenEye development: "Ady Smith Interview" in Arcade Attack (2018): https://bit.ly/2YBRuvs; "Q&A Julian Widdows" in *Edge* (issue 220, 2010); Brittany Vincent's "What's the Klobb Got to Do, Got to Do with *GoldenEye 007*'s Design Secrets" in Destructoid (2014): https://bit.ly/381b9sn; "The *GoldenEye* Arms Reference" (2002): https://bit.ly/2qpNYqH; and *Nintendo Power* (vol. 93, 1997): https://bit.ly/2pCvti6.

The Men with the Golden Guns

Eric Garrett's "*GoldenEye 007* Was Originally More Like *Time Crisis*" on Comic Book.com (2019): https://bit.ly/2MTYsWI; "TIL that the entire *GoldenEye 007* game on N64 is only 12 MB" on Reddit: https://bit.ly/2tcWkmP; "N64 *GoldenEye 007* Retro Review" in Casually Hardcore (2011): https://

bit.ly/2tv25gi; Alex Baldwin's "*GoldenEye* 64's Inspirational Startup Story" at Alexbaldwin.com: https://bit.ly/32pLeHH; "Debate: Is *GoldenEye 64* Actually An Arcade Game?" in Retro Collect (2015); and *Nintendo Power* (vol. 85, 1996): https://bit.ly/2RYdq1A.

Anti-Game Design

Tim Hong's "Shoot to Thrill: Bio-Sensory Reactions to 3D Shooting Games" in Game Developer (2008): https://ubm.io/2myYsm9; "24 *Goldeneye 007* Facts, Trivia and Cut Content Bits" YouTube video (2016): https://bit.ly/2Mzn4VT; Christian Nutt's "Interview: Zoonami's Hollis On *Bonsai Barber*'s WiiWare Sprouting" in Game Developer (2009): https://bit.ly/2S90G8J; "10 Things You Might Not Know About *Goldeneye 007* (Nintendo 64)" in Warped Factor (2019): https://bit.ly/367idCA; Chris Deleon's "Anti-Design / Backwards Game Design in *GoldenEye 007*" in *Videogame Developer's Strategy Guide* (2012); "Practical Guide on First-Person Level Design" in Medium (2017): https://bit.ly/2ohyGmP; Dalton Cooper's "The 5 Best Video Games Based on Movies" in Game Rant (2015): https://bit.ly/2OLOOIy; Jonathan Gray's *Show Sold Separately: Promos, Spoilers, and Other Media Paratexts* (2010); and "The Secrets of *GoldenEye*'s AI Revealed" on YouTube (2019): https://bit.ly/2QbymBq.

From Twycross with Love

Lawrence Fisher's "Nintendo Delays Introduction of Ultra 64 Video-Game Player" in *The New York Times* (1995): https://nyti.ms/2SqVBsc; Brad Stone's "Nintendo's Hot Box" in *Newsweek* (1996); Aaron Curtiss's "New Nintendo 64 is a

Technical Wonder" in the *Los Angeles Times* (1996): https://lat.ms/38BavCd; "Nintendo Wakes Up" in the *Economist* (1996); "Top 25 Consoles" in IGN: https://bit.ly/2nzkOns; Evan Amos's *The Game Console: A Photographic History from Atari to Xbox* (No Starch Press 2018); Levi Buchanan's "Nintendo 64 Week: Day Two" in IGN (2008): https://bit.ly/31QVaK4; Marilyn Gillen's "It's All in the Games" in *Billboard* (1994); "A Brief History of the Nintendo 64 in 1997" in Game_Tyrant: https://bit.ly/395oEr1; David Kushner's "Nintendo Grows Up and Goes for the Gross-Out" in the *New York Times* (2001): https://nyti.ms/2mKFadj; Scott Taves's "Killer Op" in *Wired* (1999): https://bit.ly/33HaM3i; Bobby Schweizer's "Difficulty" in *Debugging Game History* (MIT Press, 2016); "An Interview with Ken Lobb" in Hardcore Gaming 101 (2012): https://bit.ly/2F5WC1x; Daniel Boutros's "Difficulty Is Difficult: Designing for Hard Modes in Games" in Game Developer (2008): https://ubm.io/2mJOnCO; "Nintendo 64 (N64) Secrets & Censorship - Did You Know Gaming?" on YouTube (2019): https://bit.ly/39mFqml; Brian Ashcraft's "Japan's Gamers are Starting to Shoot 'Em Up" in the *Japan Times* (2012): https://bit.ly/2YgeW1l; Matthew Byrd's "Does Nintendo Only Care About Japan?" in Den of Geek (2017): https://bit.ly/2XgcTKE; "Iwata Asks : Link's Crossbow Training" on Nintendo.com: https://bit.ly/36ceaoK; Michael Baskett's "Japan's 1960's Spy Boom" in *James Bond and Popular Culture,* ed. by Michele Brittany (McFarland & Company, 2014); Consolevariations.com: https://bit.ly/3vKjDj3; Stephen Totilo's "The History of Headshots, Gaming's Favorite Act Of Unreal Violence" in Kotaku (2010): https://bit.ly/2BqlG1g; and Patrick Klepek's "Nintendo Wanted *GoldenEye* To End With You Shaking Everyone's Hands" in Kotaku (2015): https://bit.ly/2J6GUWg.

Slappers Only

"*GoldenEye*: The Gold Standard" in The Completionist (2020): https://bit.ly/2TzZyer; "*GoldenEye 007*" in Super Chart Island (2020): https://bit.ly/2Tyat8w; Mark Beaumont's "Why *GoldenEye 007* Is Still One of the Greatest Video Games Ever" in NME (2017): https://bit.ly/2T11r25; Botwood Twitter; "How Did *GoldenEye*'s Multiplayer Grow from a Single Paragraph of a 10 Page Design Document?" in MCV (2018): https://bit.ly/2SImk4b; Kate Cox's "Long Lost Emulation Easter Egg Discovered in *GoldenEye*" in Kotaku (2012): https://bit.ly/2VRrKcF; Kate Cox's "The Team That Made *GoldenEye* Was All For Adding That Famous Multiplayer Last Minute—They Just Didn't Tell Their Bosses" in Kotaku (2012): https://bit.ly/2pz7bWw; Joseph Walter's "25 Amazing Things Deleted From *GoldenEye 007* (That Would Have Changed Everything)" in TheGamer (2018): https://bit.ly/31Aj3oB; Jason Wojnar's "N64: 10 Hidden Details You Missed In *GoldenEye 007*" in Game Rant (2019): https://bit.ly/341MotD; Ryan Engstrom's "Retro Review: *GoldenEye 007*" in Game Tyrant (2016): https://bit.ly/2py2gVS; C.J. Andriessen's "20 Years Later, *GoldenEye 007* is Still the Greatest Nintendo 64 Game" in Destructoid (2017): https://bit.ly/35KJzP6; Cecilia D'Anastasio's "If You Hear Someone Getting Harassed in an Online Game, Don't Stay Silent" in Kotaku (2017): https://bit.ly/3tuI4zU; Cecilia D'Anastasio's "*Overwatch*'s Competitive Mode Is Depressing Right Now" in Kotaku (2017): https://bit.ly/3bTisXp; "'One in Two' Young Online Gamers Bullied, Report Finds" at the BBC (2017): https://bbc.in/3bT9ZDp; and Meg Fryling, Jami Cotler, Jack Rivituso, Lauren Mathews, and Shauna Pratico's "Cyberbullying or Normal Game Play? Impact of Age, Gender, and Experience on Cyberbullying in Multi-Player Online Gaming Environments: Perceptions from

One Gaming Forum" in the *Proceedings of the Conference for Information Systems Applied Research* (2014).

Killer App

"E3 1997 Guide" in IGN (2012): https://bit.ly/2Xobpyh; "Rare Didn't Want to Make *GoldenEye 007*, thought it would Be a Disaster, Nintendo Suggested Cancelling the Game" in Nintendo Everything (2010): https://bit.ly/352vrz5; *Multimedia Wire*'s "VSDA's Top 10 Renting Video Games" report series; *Consumer Multimedia Report*'s "Top 5 Videogame Rentals"; Joel Easley's "Annihilate Your Enemies and Get the Girl, Too" in the *Knoxville News-Sentinel* (1997); Steve Traiman's "Two Video-Game Value Series Spike Sales" in *Billboard* (1999); Taneli Palola's "Greatest Video Game Composers: Graeme Norgate - Article" in VGChartz (2018): https://bit.ly/37kSZko; Robert Crandall and J. Gregory Sidak's "Video Games: Serious Business for America's Economy" from the Entertainment Software Association (2006): https://bit.ly/2qEuU8l; Chi Kong Lui's "*GoldenEye 007*: Review" on Gamecritics.com (1998); N64.com; Robert Marrujo's "Nintendo 64 Sales on the Rise in the Secondary Market" in Nintendojo (2019): https://bit.ly/3t-k8XGx; Bill Provick's "*Goldeneye 007* Excellent, Like Starring in a Bond Film" in the *Ottawa Ctizen* (1997): https://bit.ly/36ZCxae; Scott Taves's "Live and Let Die" in *Wired* (1998): https://bit.ly/32Cc2F6; Scott Taves's "Street Cred: Live and Let Die" in *Wired* (1998): https://bit.ly/31wJono; and Doug Perry's "*GoldenEye 007* Review" in IGN (1997): https://bit.ly/2o007Sb.

Tomorrow Never Dies

"Interview with Brett Jones of SciFi Ball" on YouTube (2019): https://bit.ly/2FlSP0p; "Free Speech" in Arcade (2000);

Josh Wise's "*TimeSplitters* Creator Interview: *GoldenEye, Future Perfect*, and the Koch Media Acquisition" in Video Gamer (2018): https://bit.ly/2F7Or4S; Rich Stanton's "Free Radical vs. The Monsters" in Eurogamer (2012): https://bit.ly/2ZHnr5B; Stephany Nunneley's "Free Radical–Battlefront 3 Cancelled by 'Psychopaths' at LucasArts" in VG247 (2012): https://bit.ly/3GS8fqS; Damien McFerran's "*GoldenEye 007* Director Martin Hollis Found a Weakness In The N64 That Almost Caused Another Delay" in Nintendo Life (2016): https://bit.ly/2MZL70b; Jez Corden's "*Sea of Thieves* Creator Rare's Studio is a Magical (and Unforgettable) Place" in Windows Central (2018): https://bit.ly/37ovMho; Xander Markham's "15 Year Anniversary Retrospective: *GoldenEye 007* (N64, 1997)" in Game Developer: https://bit.ly/2Or5e7Y; Emily Gera's "*GoldenEye* Director Unveiling Experimental Matchmaking Game *Aim for Love* at GameCity" in Kotaku (2013): https://bit.ly/2oWxjdR; Matthew Reynolds's "*GoldenEye* Creator Martin Hollis on His Experimental Game *Aim for Love*" in Kotaku (2013): https://bit.ly/35PhdTQ; Stephen Totilo's "'Make Love Games, Not War Games,' Says Former First-Person Shooter Creator" in Kotaku (2012): https://bit.ly/2P6fALF; "Brett Jones" Mandy profile; Duncan Botwood LinkedIn; Shawn Laib's "An Interview with Legendary Composer Grant Kirkhope" in Super Jump (2020): https://bit.ly/39DLj1h; and Steve Ellis's LinkedIn.

ACKNOWLEDGMENTS

THANK YOU FIRST AND FOREMOST to Gabe Durham and Michael P. Williams for their support of this project from the very beginning, and for their brilliant editorial feedback and research notes every step along the way. I'm also grateful to Joe M. Owens and Nick Sweeney for their eagle-eyed proof-reading and copy editing, and to Chris Moyer, Cory Schmitz, and Mel Tow for their beautiful design work.

Thank you very much to the members of the original *GoldenEye* development team who so generously shared their memories from the era with me: Duncan Botwood, David Doak, Mark Edmonds, Steve Ellis, Karl Hilton, Brett Jones, Grant Kirkhope, Graeme Norgate, and Ady Smith. I'm also very grateful to the gaming and Bond experts who shared their expertise with me: Harper Jay MacIntyre, Chris Groves, Stefan Hall, Brian Hamaker, Simon Parkin, John Romero, Jeremy Strong, Nicolás Suszczyk, Carl Therrien, Martin Watts, and Logan West.

I would like to extend a heartfelt thanks to the following individuals for sharing with me their personal memories of *GoldenEye*: Jonathan Baran, Tim Bednar, Cayla Bellamy, Ben

Bever, Hayley Button, Sara Portoghese Channing, Jeb Cooke, Alec Garcia, Nic Glumsic, Sara Florence Huff, RJ Ingram, Brandon Katz, Julie Kenneally, Jamie Klingensmith, Kendal Lotze, Rachael Lussos, David McDonald, Rich Neal, Jorge Palacios Jr., Jeff Rickel, Chris Roberts, Nathan Rode, Taylor Rushing, Madeline Shaughnessy, Matt Taylor, Ben Wilkins, Colby Pierce Wortham, Philip Yero, and Elder Zamora. For all the wonderful *GoldenEye* memories of my own, thank you to Conor Britain, John McMillian, and Erin Barnett.

I deeply appreciate the support of my colleagues in the Regis University English Department, as well as the resources provided by the Regis library and interlibrary loan. I am also grateful to Chris Roberts, Regis's Faculty Development Committee, and Regis's Undergraduate Research and Scholarship Council for providing grant funding to make this work possible.

Thank you to Lynetta Mier, Erin Winterrowd, Robin Hextrum, Kayla Sargent, Diana Schmertz, Mel Nichols, Siwar Masannat, Ellie Brigida, Leesa Charlotte, and Olivia Tracy for their warmth and friendship during the writing period, and to Derek Parks for taking me to the shooting range to compare real-life shooting to *GoldenEye* shooting. For help translating research materials from French to English, and for all of her encouragement during the writing process, a big thank-you to Alison McCarthy.

Finally, thank you to Kate Partridge for always believing in me, for supporting me at every turn, and for spending several years listening to way too many *GoldenEye* facts.

ALSO FROM
BOSS FIGHT BOOKS